S^AND^^) LOAN

Getting Gigs!
The Musician's and Singer's Survival Guide
to Booking Better Paying Jobs

D1614983

Getting Gigs!
The Musician's and Singer's Survival Guide to Booking Better Paying Jobs

With or Without An Agent

By Mark W. Curran

ISBN 978-0-9706773-2-7
2nd Edition 2010

Publisher: NMD Books - 2828 Cochran St. Suite 285 - Simi Valley, CA. 93065
Retail: $19.95
Category: Reference/Music Marketing
Perfect bound

A comprehensive guide to finding the best paying gigs for musicians and singers, from their local area to the international stage. A music business veteran gives the inside track to creating a profitable career in the performing arts, from local clubs international cruise ships. Includes interviews with successful musicians and entertainment directors who share their secrets in landing the best paying gigs. Also includes directories of resources for further research.

 Typeset and printed by Stallion Press
Email: sales@stallionpress.com

Table of Contents

Introduction

This book is the result of thirty-plus years of paying my dues as a professional musician, singer and recording artist, and a career path that continues to this day. This experience includes traveling extensively throughout the United States with acts ranging from hard rock bands to being a solo artist with an acoustic guitar, singing originals, to becoming, in my mid-forties, of all things, a professional Elvis Impersonator, based in Los Angeles.

This book approaches the subject of gigging from the grass-roots level, aimed at "no-name," unknown local performers who are ready to go out and play locally and start making money doing what they love. It also allows for growth by showing you how you can take your act from a local level to a national one, and beyond.

I've picked up quite a few insights, tips and tricks along the way that I know a musician or performer of any age in any pursuit of a career in performing live music can use to great advantage. Although the kinds of music being played change, as it always has, the rules of the game remain fundamentally the same. But the playing field itself has undergone radical changes.

The live music business has changed tremendously in the last twenty years. The shift from live club music to more specialized venues has made the market for live music much more competitive.

In the seventies and well into the eighties, a musician could work six nights a week at the local Holiday Inn or Ramada Inn lounge, even book a cross country tour of the lounge circuit and gig for as many months as they desired.

Sadly, it seems, those days are over.

A vast number of lounges have closed down due to economics, drinking laws, insurance liability, and just plain bottom line cuts. This slide began back in the mid to late eighties, and I have not seen any major shift back from this market condition. But that does not mean the end.

Market conditions, the economy, shifting social trends, all play an important role in any given business. And the music business is after all, a business selling a product.

Technology has played a big role in the way people get entertainment.

People have more options on where to spend their entertainment dollars. With the advancement of home entertainment systems and computers, digital satellite television and other diversions, as well as the trend toward a healthier lifestyle (non-alcoholic), it seems the lounges have seen their heyday.

In many ways, the going is a lot tougher than it used to be for the gigging musician. National "name" acts, backed by corporate dollars and conglomerate-owned radio stations, dominate the local markets at any given time, making it even harder for a local act to attract a following.

Advertising has gotten so expensive as to be often cost prohibitive for a local act to attract people to their shows, and flyers announcing such shows have to be distributed in such large numbers as to make them only marginally cost effective.

However grim the outlook on playing local clubs, there are many opportunities where the well-informed and motivated musician can find or create work. This book explores and outlines these opportunities, and provides a roadmap to follow.

In fact, I discourage acts from trying to get gigs where all the other acts are trying to get gigs, and encourage the resourceful performer "to go where no other performer has gone before," opening up new vistas for performing, and even creating a few of their own. Easy? No way. Challenging? Yes, infinitely. But with being in charge of your own gigs, empowerment will liberate you from the tyranny of ruthless dictators.

Keep in mind that all the ideas and secrets in the world are inert unless put into action, and thus lies the secret and hidden challenge to all self-help books. These principles and techniques are only as good as you are at working them, and they are effective only if you apply them on a consistent basis. This is not an easy task, but then, this isn't an easy business. (What business is?)

You are well advised to put a realistic business plan together and to follow a step-by-step process to accomplishing your goals.

This book will show you not where and how to find the gigs, but how to create your own, and to look for gigs in places nobody else is looking. In the final analysis, it is up to you to put in the work required to see results.

In my research and consulting work with musicians, the single biggest deterrent to their success seems to be the musicians themselves. Over and over, the single biggest factor I see as their essential flaw is that many desire success but few do the work necessary to achieve it.

In the fierce, competitive world of music, perseverance and hard work are of great necessity. It often requires an investment of dollars and time and a great deal of effort to see results. It is here where many musicians fail.

But for the determined few willing to put in what is required, the rewards are great.

Unlike many books about the music business, what this book will not do is paint a unrealistic, rosy colored view of the music business. My approach to the subject is that it's a tough way to make living, and it is. If my views seem a little negative or tough, it's only because this is what I've found to be true.

The thing I find most bothersome about books on making it in music is that they often assume you are just going to go out and do a few things and the whole thing will fall in your lap. They assume your calls will be returned, they assume your following will build, and so on.

I think it's a disservice to people to write books on things which have not been proven in the author's experience to be true. The things I detail in this book have been experienced by myself and also in the trusted judgement and experience of my colleagues, whom were carefully chosen to be interviewed for this book.

In the end, this book will not go out and get you work. What you will achieve will only come through tough-skin and hard work.

But through the difficulty, the business of music is one of the most rewarding and exciting occupations in the world.

Few other jobs exist that offer more in terms of fun, travel, meeting new people, and money. Few jobs offer as much satisfaction as seeing an audience experiencing pure joy from your talent.

As a side note, this book has been written with equal consideration to both musicians and singers, and so for the sake a brevity, wherever I refer to "act" or "musician," I am also targeting those singers who are reading this book with an eye toward advancing their singing careers, either with a backing band, or as a solo act.

Simply put, this book is your most valuable tool in achieving success as a gigging musician.

Use it to prosper and discover your innermost self.

Mark W. Curran
Los Angeles, CA.

CHAPTER 1

The Basics

State of Business, Then and Now

The state of the music business today as it pertains to the gigging musician is as stated in the introduction, much different than it was twenty years ago. But there are many places to play. Overall, the market has continued to evolve, and with that evolution, new opportunities have opened up.

One dismaying aspect of today's music world is that it is becoming dominated by corporate America. Large conglomerates are monopolizing the concert, recording and radio business. These large behemoths are not developing new talent but are packaging and repackaging existing signed acts, which means that many local musicians are denied a shot at playing large venues.

Although this is largely a phenomenon that is affecting touring acts playing larger venues, it still has great impact for the future of live music. When several large companies

7

control much of the music the general public gets to hear, it is not a good thing.

The cruise lines are providing more work for full time musicians than they ever have, with new ships being built every year. This rapidly expanding market has overtaken all others as one of the primary sources of work for musicians.

Colleges are another expanding market showing healthy growth. Fairs continue to expand as well as the newly emerging phenomenon of house concerts.

The market is better than ever for the motivated musician to find gigs.

What It Takes to Succeed

First and foremost, you need a goal, with clearly defined steps on how to achieve this goal. Where do you want to be five years from now? Do you desire to be in a national act, touring and recording? Or is your goal to be working part-time on the weekends playing top 40 at the local club?

Whatever your goal, write it down.

Then write down the possible steps you will need to take in order to achieve that goal.

What it takes to succeed in the music business is perseverance, meaning you must stick to your guns and work diligently each day to achieve your goal, no matter what obstacles are placed in your way.

Rejection is something you will be faced with daily. Learn to put your emotions aside when dealing with the hard economics of the music business, and not take rejection personally. Rejection is usually tied to economics, and the laws of supply and demand, so don't let it bother you.

You are in a business where so many others like yourself are trying to get the same job. In such a business, rejection is going to happen. Ignore it and move on.

If you continue to plug away at your goal regardless of rejection, you will find yourself at the next level of development. For most people will eventually give up after enough rejection. It is the person willing to persevere in the face of adversity who will succeed.

The single biggest mistake I see is that most musicians will not invest in themselves, meaning they tend to go the path of least resistance. It takes work, money and a lot of gumption to get ahead in any business, and in one like music, it is harder than most.

Invest in the tools you need to make a success of yourself. That means arming yourself with information (books), having marketing materials printed, sending out mailings, making phone calls, shooting videos and photos, the list goes on and on.

Don't go the cheap route: your image is everything. Dress for success, market hard and often, and stay in front of your prospects; and remember the ABC's of marketing and sales: Always Be Closing.

Making the Big Bucks

Although money can be a prime motivator, it should not be the only objective. Most musicians play music out of a passionate desire to express themselves through music, and to entertain other people.

Kevin Eubanks of the Tonight Show Band has said he never went after better gigs because of the money, he chose gigs that would improve him as a musician first, and the money would usually follow.

There's a lot of money to be made as a gigging musician, but also look at how a gig is going to better you as a player and as a person. Helping others with your music through playing a benefit can sometimes be far more rewarding than a paying gig. This is only one example, but I think you can see my point.

The Shangri-La Illusion

Here's a phenomenon that affects a lot of players, and if it isn't kept under control, can create a lot of misery. It's called "The Shangri-La Illusion," and it's the misconception that there is an ideal gig somewhere over the rainbow that is going to be hassle free and will result in happiness beyond your wildest dreams.

There is no such gig.

I knew a musician who was unhappy with his marriage, and after being laid off from his job, he decided to take a job on a cruise ship. This particular cruise line did not pay very well, but he figured he would be able to save money and have the time of his life doing it.

He packed up all his stuff and put it into storage, sold his car, left his wife, and went aboard the cruise ship for what he thought was going to be at least a year. He figured this was going to be a paid vacation for him, an endless party of girls, exotic locales and a Shangri-La.

About one week into this gig, he realized he had been entirely wrong about the cruise ship gig. Cut off from civilization, unable to communicate with his family, he spent many sleepless nights in a cramped cabin in the dark bowels of the ship.

He found his co-workers were not friendly, he was not allowed to talk to the passengers, and the rules and regulations of living on a ship, coupled with the stress he encountered dealing with a very difficult orchestra leader took its toll. Added to this the loneliness and isolation he encountered, he began drinking heavily, and soon his misery was apparent to everyone around him, including the cruise director, who promptly sent him home.

Had he been realistic about his expectations of the cruise ship gig, and had he done his research by talking to musicians who had worked this type of gig, he would have realized this gig was not for him. His Shangri-La Illusion would have been put into perspective, and he would not have taken the job. Every gig has its problems as well as its benefits. Before assuming there is a hassle free gig coming down the pike, know that the hassle free gig does not exist.

Timing is Everything

Trends and styles of music evolve, but nothing is more influential on a musician's career than the state of the economy. Economic growth and change tends to go in seven-year cycles, meaning that every seven years or so, we experience recession.

This has a large impact on gigs, since people tend to cut their entertainment dollars first. If you are trying to get your gigging business off the ground in a difficult economic time, understand it will be more difficult to land jobs.

By contrast, when we are in an upward swing in the economy, jobs will be easier to land. During these periods, save your money, for without fail, the cycle will repeat itself. Real estate professionals know this all too well, and plan for it in advance.

In a similar way, the type and style of music you play and its current popularity can dictate your success level, for the type of music enjoying current popularity will be more sought out by buyers.

I remember during the rockabilly boom just after the Stray Cats broke worldwide, all the clubs and buyers wanted rockabilly groups.

Should this dictate the type of music you play?

Not necessarily, but understand it can have an impact on your bottom line.

Agents

Do you need an agent? The fast answer is, no.

In today's local gig market, the average act is rarely, if ever represented by an agent.

There was a time when an agent would "go to bat" for his acts, make calls, and really hustle to get a group work.

But now it seems agents feel it's far easier to let the work come to them. Since there are so many more acts than there are jobs, the law of supply and demand again dictates protocol.

What many of today's agents have become are order takers, waiting for the phone to ring from buyers who tell the agents the type of act they want, and the agent goes through his files to find the right act for the right job.

What this means is that every agent you call (or any other person who can book you) will likely request your package, and then file that material away for the unlikely time they get a call for your type of group. This "file and forget it" order taking mentality simply reduces agents to middlemen who care very little about your welfare or getting you work.

If you send your complete package including a video and include your postage and follow up calls, you are spending at least $5–$8 per package. Sending that out to 100 agents is $500–$800, so measure your results carefully.

You may have the right act for the right time, in an area where there is great demand for your type of music. Hooking up with a well-connected agent in this situation could result in steady full time work.

But speaking in general terms, again, you will likely get far more work on your own in today's market than an agent will ever get you.

You may find an agent that really loves your act and really wants to get you work, and he might make calls on your behalf, but this kind of thing has gone the way of the service station attendant that used to check your oil and wash your windshield.

My experience with agents is that no matter how good your tape or package is, there's a good chance you will not even get a follow up call from your efforts and expense, because they will likely "file and forget" you, until the unlikely time they get a call that might tickle their memory enough to search for your file.

But also remember that the sales game works on the law of averages, and the more packages you get out there, the better your chances of getting work, but don't expect much from agents.

You must offset this by taking into consideration the cost of the package verses the amount of jobs you are getting from agents.

Business Managers

If you are gigging on a local level, you will seldom require a business manager. Once you are established and playing nationally, you may find having someone taking care of your business a great asset, but do so with caution.

The business abounds with stories of rip-off managers that steal their clients money and vanish, and they aren't just stories; they're true. Many a star has woken up to the hard reality that their millions have been stolen by ruthless managers and accountants.

When do you need a manager?

Even if you reach star status, you may never need a manager, particularly if you are business minded. Many musicians are not: art and commerce rarely can co-exist peacefully.

Some of the best business manager/artist relationships occur when a spouse proves adept at business and can function in the capacity of business manager. A good example of this is Wayne Newton, whose wife is an attorney and handles all his business affairs.

Beware of people who will approach you and tell you need them as a business manager.

For whom have they performed in this capacity in the past? Do they have references? Check them out before signing any contracts, and remember, nobody can take care of your business better than you can, if you are a committed and smart businessperson.

Keep an eye on your money: if you don't it will disappear.

Your USP (Unique Selling Proposition)

Those of you who have studied marketing probably know about the USP. This is the statement you create about yourself to sell yourself to others. It should contain something unique you have to offer your prospects that exceed that of your competitors. Something that makes you stand out and makes you different.

It could be a unique look or presentation, such as matching costumes or themes, (Paul revere And The Raiders) or unique characters (Kiss, David Bowie as Ziggy Stardust).

In order to compete in a crowded market, you need an edge, and that edge is your uniqueness. If you specialize in a certain genre or style of music, your USP could be that you do it in a style or present it in a way that is different from similar bands or acts competing in your area.

It is not enough to merely say you do it better. This is simply rhetoric to people who want to hire you. You must prove to them you do it better, and show them the results of doing it better.

If you have a larger following than your competitors as a result of doing it better, and you want to land a gig, you might show the buyer your mailing list, or give them references of people who have hired you that can vouch for your credibility and the fact you can draw 300 people to your events.

Take the time to develop your USP, and use it in your pitch to agents and buyers, both verbal and printed.

One local band in Los Angeles is a Steely Dan Tribute, and their musicianship is outstanding. Their USP is:

"We are the only Steely Dan Tribute Act in Los Angeles that can play Steely Dan just like the record, and we have a local following that is very dedicated to showing up at all of our events."

Strategy and Implementation

Getting Gigs is a matter of strategy and implementation. The first step is to develop your goal; the next step is to develop a marketing and sales strategy that will help you accomplish that goal.

The third, most important step is to actually implement the strategy, meaning, "Put it to work."

Each day you must commit to your strategy, making phone calls, working the Internet, sending out promo packages, faxing, and making personal visits to your prospects. The single biggest factor that stands in the way of success and failure is the inability to develop a strategy, and the unwillingness to implement it.

Sounds simple, doesn't it?

But many times the diametric opposites of music and business make strange bedfellows. You must consistently learn to budget your time between business and practice, or one will suffer at the expense of the other.

Its tough being immersed in difficult business transactions and the stress and pressure of performance, and then have to switch it all off and go into practice mode, where all your concentration and energy are needed to not do business.

But these opposite functions must co-exist in an as disciplined manner as possible.

One way to accomplish this is to devote a certain time frame each day for business, and the other time frame for practice. It could be done on an hourly basis, or set aside mornings for practice, the afternoons for business. Try to do this the same times each day to establish the behavioral pattern.

When practicing, turn off the phone and try to be in a space where you will not be disturbed by outside noise, people, or demands. Know that when your practice time is up you'll be able to address whatever needs your attention then.

Longevity

There is much to be said for staying in the game for the long haul. Few things of value can be accomplished over the short term. If you've decided you want to be a successful musician, prepare to be in it for years, not months.

To insure your longevity, take care of yourself. Self-destructiveness is common in the arts. Drinking and drugs will only reduce your effectiveness, sap your energy and create problems for you.

The true success stories in music involve careers that span decades, not years.

CHAPTER 2

Tools

Computer
Internet and Website
Database
Card File
Telephone
Fax
Mail

What You Need to Make It

A computer is most essential in this day and age. On it you will be able to compose letters, store databases, print mailing labels, and cruise the web for job leads and information.

Home computers have come down in price in recent years and can be bought on the used market for pennies on the dollar. I would recommend a PC of at least 486 mhz, with at least 10 gigs of hard drive, with a 56 K modem or higher speed LAN connection.

Your Internet connection can something as simple as America Online to something as optimal as high speed DSL or cable modem access. The great advantage to a higher speed connection is that images and downloads will be much faster than with a dial up connection.

The time you will save (not to mention the frustration) is well worth the extra money.

In terms of software, a database program can be very helpful. In it you can organize names, addresses, phone/fax numbers, emails and notes. Some of the more sophisticated database programs such as Goldmine include autodialers, calendars and schedulers that can make prospecting and follow ups a real breeze.

A great free Database and Contact Management Program software is called *Contact Plus.*

Their website can be found at *http://www.contactplus.com*

Another handy tool to have in your arsenal is a standard 3 × 5 index card file, which can be purchased at any office supply store. Buy a box of index cards and organize all of your contacts on these cards. You will find this immensely helpful when making calls and your computer is turned off, or if you need to reference something quickly and don't want to wait for your computer to reboot. It also makes a handy backup should you forget to backup your hard drive!

Telephone

This is your best friend. Make calls and make them often. Your prospect list should be in constant motion: either being called on or scheduled for a "tickler" (reminder) call that you or your act is available and taking bookings.

Staying in touch with your prospects, be they clubs, corporate, agents or otherwise, is the only way to stay fresh in the minds of your potential customers.

Fax

The fax machine is also an essential tool. Make "Info Faxes" of your acts description, prices, and availability, out-lining your USP. ("Unique Selling Proposition.") Use this fax when calling your prospects. When they may have a hard time remembering your group, package or music, offer to fax them a "reminder" of your pricing and act so that they can "file" it away.

There are also computer programs that can work in tandem with your contact database management software that will allow you to send an instant fax while you are talking on the phone with them.

Mail

Direct mail is expensive and time consuming. But it can be approached in a creative way. A "reminder" postcard in full color can be printed and mailed for less than $.75 each, and can be an effective sales tool. Keep careful records of your results to determine if direct mail is working for your act.

CHAPTER 3

Packaging and Selling Your Act

YOU are the Product—Make It Count

When packaging and selling your act, keep in mind that first and foremost, YOU are the product. Always use your uniqueness and personality when contacting people, and make your individuality shine through. Here are a number of tools for you to use in packaging and selling your act.

Internet and Website

In today's high tech world, a website is an absolute must. More and more people are turning to the Internet to find musicians and acts, for all types of events. You will need at least a basic website, designed for easy navigation, that clearly states the type of act you are, where you are based, the services you offer and the types of clients you service.

Photos, audio and video samples, and a price range is also helpful. Make sure you have a phone number published on the website in large numbers. An email address is also very helpful, but you'd be surprised at how many band websites don't include all this basic information.

It is also essential your site is coded with the proper keywords and metatags that will insure your listing will appear on all the major search engines, especially Google.

There are many small companies that can help you with building and maintaining a website, and the cost is minimal.

Make sure to include in your website an email list where people can join to receive updates on where you are appearing, and the latest news on your recordings. You can also set up an online store where you can sell merchandise such as CD's, t-shirts and other marketing tools.

In addition to having your own website, another phenomenon of web booking that is starting to emerge are sites that send you leads for gigs in your area. The idea behind this is a company sets itself up as a go-between for people looking to hire acts and the acts themselves. You pay several dollars for the lead or you pay several dollars to bid on the job. Listings of these sites appear in the appendix section. By the time you read this, there may be many more.

Personally, I have not booked any jobs from these gigfinder-style services, the ones I have joined seem to be looking for entertainment for children's parties, top 40 bands, or acoustic guitarists, but I think this situation will change as more companies get into the act.

Marketing yourself and music on the internet is an advanced level subject full of complexity, which I have covered in detail in my book "Sell Your Music," available from my website and from the order form included in the back of this book.

The Press Kit—And Why It Will Most Likely Not Get You Work

The big problem with a press kit is that you need one, but nine times out of ten it won't get you work. I've found that when people request a press kit they are usually not serious about buying your act. I know this runs contrary to popular belief, but after sending hundreds of press kits out over the years, I've found it to be true.

Whether or not the press kit gets you work, you are still going to need one, and in order to knock down the first roadblock people will put in your way when they say they are considering booking you.

A press kit should contain:

- An 8 × 10 black and white glossy photo of your act, professionally taken
- A bio and history of your act, with a Unique Selling Proposition
- An edited 5 minute video of your act that is exciting and impressive
- A list of venues worked, and at least three references and testimonials
- Clippings of any news articles that have run on your act
- Your contact information, including website and phone/fax numbers

A lot of times, clubs and prospects request that you send them something because that is an easy way to get you off the phone. But you must send it, or try to get them to view your EPK, as described here:

What I have done is to put up an "Electronic Press Kit" (EPK) on my website which includes a bio, streaming audio and video, press clippings and photos. The difficulty with an EPK is that some of your prospects will not even want to take the time to go to your website. But my thought on this is that if someone is not willing to take the time to go to your website, are they really that serious about hiring you?

Some of your prospects may not have fast enough Internet connections to accommodate your streaming video. In a case like this, I'd send the press kit, but try to qualify your prospect. A press kit can cost up to $10 a pop to send one you add it all up, so be selective to whom you send it to, and make sure to always follow up.

Photos

Photos are vitally important. This is no place to cut corners. A professional photo is your most important tool, next to your video. Contact a professional photographer in your area and take a look at his/her work.

What you are looking for is a photo that captures the essence of your act. Live performance photos as well as headshots can be taken and placed into creative composites. Try to go for at least one photo that conveys excitement and movement.

Videos

This is the most important tool of all in your sales arsenal. You need a live performance video that has been edited to no longer than five minutes, with different camera angles in front of an enthusiastic live audience.

I've found the best way to do this is to do it in a club or small theater, and invite as many friends and members of the public for free to attend. You can get great deals on video taping from a local college.

Many colleges and adult extension courses offer classes in ideography/ editing. Often these classes search for events to videotape as class assignments. You may be able to get a free video done for your act using this method.

There are also many wedding videographers in your area who can assist you in videotaping your performance. Consult your yellow pages for listings.

Another method for getting a free videotape of your performance is to contact your local cable television station. Every community has a public access channel with studio facilities available for use by the general public.

By applying for their producer program, you can sign up with the TV production facility to schedule a performance to be videotaped in their studio. They will supply the crew, equipment and lighting, and will switch the cameras "live" as you perform.

The only difficulty with this is that the lighting conditions in the studios tend to look rather flat, and it is difficult to get a studio audience together unless you have lots of friends. If you can get a creative lighting director and can gather at least fifty people for your audience, the public access method might just work for you.

One more benefit to this method is that the station will also cablecast your performance on their public access channel, which reaches members of their service area.

You can also take your taped performance to other cable stations in surrounding areas and schedule it for cablecasting. You may not get huge exposure, but it's a great way to get free advertising for your act.

Cards

Business cards are essential. Again, don't cut corners. Have a professional card designed and printed, preferably in full color. Make sure that you have a card that is so well designed, people will keep it. Give your cards out to everyone, and don't skimp on giving them out. They are your cheapest form of advertising.

Person To Person

Nothing beats person-to-person contact when selling your act, particularly to clubs. It's hard to ignore someone who is standing in your doorway, and the personal contact forges a memorable bond that works wonders when you follow up with a phone call.

Many people who hire acts are busy, so you really have to be diplomatic in how you approach them. It's often best to try to approach with a phone call first, a mailing second, and then a personal appearance if your calls are not answered.

CHAPTER 4

Personal Inventory

Personality

We've all heard it and experienced it: Musicians can be temperamental, unstable characters, ego driven, difficult to work with. But many have overcome these difficulties by developing a professional attitude when it comes to doing business in the music world.

Ego is something that will rarely help you as a musician, except as a foil to project confidence. But those who need to go on an ego trip to project such confidence are operating in a self-deceptive world that is often transparent to others.

We all bring to the table our own share of personal problems. By taking a personal inventory, you can identify possible problems before they become a hindrance to your musical career.

A personal inventory is a list of grievances and resentments you may have accumulated over your lifetime, both past and present. By writing these down, you may find that your attitude and personality reflect inner conflicts you may have not been consciously aware of.

Twelve step programs use the method of taking a personal inventory as a step toward recovery from addictive, destructive behaviors that cause conflicts in business and personal living. It can be used effectively for identifying if we indeed "carry a chip on our shoulders" over some past real or imagined wrong.

Your personality is one of the most important factors in your success as a musician. When dealing with people, always project a positive, cooperative manner that is inclusive of the other person's concerns. When booking jobs, you are providing a service, let the person know you understand that. A little bit of compassion goes a long way!

This same understanding, patience, and positive outlook should also be used when dealing with fellow musicians. One of the biggest causes of conflict within music groups is personality and ego driven quests for power.

If these trips can be identified and eliminated for the greater good of a common cause, which is making great music and booking better gigs, then the chances of success are multiplied.

Appearance and Grooming

This is show business, and the "show" side of the equation is just as important as the "business." One's appearance and grooming should be impeccable at all times, but never is this more important when dealing with prospective clients and when performing onstage.

Being of sound mind and body, staying in good physical shape, getting the proper rest and nutrition and looking your best at all times takes work, and a lot of it. Your clothing and hair should reflect your professionalism.

Some of us are brought up to know that good grooming is important to success, some of us are not. But never do I see a more shocking negligence to grooming and dress than with musicians.

Perhaps this is an overstay from the sixties, when torn, dirty jeans and faded work shirts worn with long, unkempt greasy hair and it seemed the grungier the look, the more hip.

But today's successful musician needs to look sharp, professional, and conscientious to succeed in an ever-increasingly corporate marketplace. The music business has become much more of a business in the past twenty years, and the drive is on for acts that reflect that professionalism.

Of course, you need not feel obligated to wear custom made suits when applying for gigs at clubs, and your look is going to be dictated by the circumstances and the nature of your act.

But by and large, you should dress (and smell) successful, reasonably fashionable, reflecting a casual elegance.

Both onstage and off, dress for success!

Health

It may seem a given to take great lengths to take care of your health, many musicians do not. Often, musicians will forsake a regular diet and exercise program and it is a big mistake. The only way to insure optimum performance in all aspects of your life is to keep your weight at a healthy level, get plenty of rest and exercise, eat healthy foods, and drink lots of water.

You are demanding a lot from your body and mind when calling upon it to perform tasks such as the stress of traveling and performing, rehearsals, keeping up on the business, and the worry of keeping food on the table.

One hour of exercise per day, five days per week, consisting of weight training and aerobics is ideal. Walking can also supplement this regimen. Joining a health club is also a great way to stay in shape, and many offer personal trainers and diet programs to fit every budget.

Larger health club chains such as Bally's 24 Hour Fitness have locations nationally and can be a great way to stay in shape, even when traveling.

Make sure you take the time to take care of your body— it is your temple and if you take care of it, it will reward you with many years of trouble-free performance.

Integrity

Personal integrity is an important aspect of your relationships with people you do business with. Being a dependable person who treats others with kindness, fairness and a value system that is complimentary will go a long way toward establishing you as a person with integrity who is honest and considerate.

This means doing what you say, and saying what you mean. It also means you pay your musicians their full promised amounts and deliver exactly what you've promised in your contractual obligations to both your musicians and to those who hire you.

Relationships and Sex

One of the biggest stumbling blocks in a musician's life is relationships, and yes, sex. Often we find ourselves exposed to large numbers of people, and as temptation is everywhere, we are sometimes approached by members of the opposite sex, more so than in other professions because we are in the public eye as performers.

The more popular your act becomes, the more you will be approached by those who are interested in exploiting you professionally and yes, even sexually.

Remember that a person who wants to go to bed with you based on your popularity on a stage does not know anything about you, they are chasing an image. While it may be fun having a one-night stand with someone who admires you from the crowd, it also has its dangers.

It's difficult maintaining a steady relationship or marriage when you are in the public eye, even on a local level, especially as musicians. But it's done all the time, if you have an exceptionally understanding "significant other" that trusts you are not going to run off with the groupies. (If you are lucky enough to have groupies, that is.)

It's heady stuff. Imagine a guy who hasn't been particularly successful with girls through high school and suddenly he is in a band that the girls go crazy over. I've seen this happen over and over, and the guy goes after every chick he can get his hands on.

But then he starts to lose focus of the music, and the business. The party life takes over. Jealousies can start within the group over girls. Girls can play games to manipulate the guys in the band. Guys can play games to manipulate the girl(s) in the band. Add drugs and drinking to this mix and you have a lethal dose of destruction, and your entire business can come crashing to the ground.

When we are young it's normal to want to have varied experiences with multiple sex partners, but keep in mind that in this day of aids and other sexually transmitted diseases, there are risks.

There is usually always the element of sexual attractiveness in the marketing and presentation of an act. It's hard to imagine Tom Jones, Guns and Roses or Brittany Spears without the allure of sexual promise.

Many musicians get into the business precisely to get the girls (or guys, as the case may be). But remember that people have emotions, and try to be responsible.

Try to use restraint over your sexual appetite, and always practice safe sex.

Bottles, Bongs and Other Roadblocks

While I don't want to go on a moral tirade here, one of the biggest roadblocks I've seen get in the way of and ultimately destroy a performer's career is drinking and drugs.

Back in the 60's and 70's it was fashionable and even expected that a performer use drugs and alcohol. This was the accepted norm. As far back as the 20's and 30's, heroin use was fashionable with jazz and blues musicians.

But times have changed, in that, we now know the health dangers inherent in their use. Aside from Ego, which we will cover next, addictions are the single biggest destroyer of lives and careers in the realm of performers that I have ever encountered.

First of all, being in clubs and bars and places where alcohol is served, we are always exposed to it, and the people who drink it. Patrons will often buy us drinks.

A few drinks seem acceptable, but I would venture that the taking of even one drink while you are working is a negative. First of all, club owners, particularly in well-heeled establishments such as major hotel chains, are watching us. Many frown on or even prohibit musicians from drinking on the job.

Outside of the gig, what you do on your own time is of course, your business. But remember that alcohol is addictive, and can lead to severe health problems. I've seen a lot of guys not only lose their careers, but their marriages and their houses, everything, all because of booze.

Drugs, even marijuana can impair judgement, create health problems, and a litany of legal entanglements that can threaten not only your own well being and career, but also those of your fellow band mates.

A word of advice:

Live your life chemical-free, and you will grow and prosper both personally and professionally.

Ego Battles

Here it is, the great destroyer of bands and careers, the single most common denominator shared by many casualties in the music business. Ego. Nothing prevents an act from moving forward more than this.

Ego, as defined by Webster's, is "an exaggerated sense of self-importance," and "an inflated feeling of pride in your superiority to others."

Ego battles occur when a personality within the band disagrees with another personality in the band, and a power struggle ensues. Many times it's over who has the most authority, or who will get more of the spotlight onstage, but the bottom line is that two parties will choose to disagree and in most cases it's a matter of ego.

Bands by their nature tend not to work very well as democracies. One leader should be designated whose final word is the final say, or endless squabbles will ensue to no beneficial end. If the person in charge is level headed and fair, the rest of the band will trust the judgement of the leader and not allow ego to get in the way.

If you are a bandleader and you are always in conflict with one particular person in your group, you may find replacing them to be your only real solution. If not, the person can create tension within the group and further conflict, which in turn will hurt your business in the long run.

But if you find yourself constantly in conflict with everyone else, you may need to re-examine your own ego. Nobody likes a ruthless dictator. Treat the people in your organization with respect and dignity, and they will return the favor by working seamlessly and selflessly with you to insure smooth and successful operation.

Ego battles also occur between band leaders and agents, managers and club owners, too. If you find yourself in endless conflict with someone who repeatedly wants to establish a power position over you and you can't resolve it, drop that person from your life. You don't need them.

Stress, Mental States and Personality Dysfunction

The business of life itself is stressful. Survival can be difficult in a world filled with conflict and bad news. Add to this our many mental states and the proliferation of personality dysfunction, it's a wonder we can get anything done at all without Prozac and other prescription remedies.

There are many people who, although not diagnosed, suffer from personality dysfunctions that are mentally or chemically based, such as depression and bi-polar disorder. Border-line schizophrenia is not as uncommon as you may think.

If you are wondering why the concert promoter you are dealing with is given to screaming and shouting rages and is abusive, perhaps he is mentally dysfunctional!

The same goes for your fellow musicians, and possibly even yourself. Understand these various mental states and conditions, because in understanding them and being made aware of them, you can deal with them more effectively.

Stress takes its toll in so many ways, and some of those ways we are not even aware of. Hypertension and high blood pressure is one of the biggest silent killers out there.

Negative mental states give way to short tempers and defeatist attitudes and are "progress killers."

Staying positive and making sure you are taking care of yourself mentally as well as physically is paramount to healthy living. Taking part in an activity or activities that you enjoy is a good practice.

Reading, hobbies, positive social interaction and meditation will help to develop a more positive mental attitude and reduce stress. Take a walk, get fresh air, and distract yourself from your everyday problems before they take their toll on your body and mind.

We can't always escape stress and be in business, but we can manage stress.

If you find yourself in a constant state of anxiety or feel tired and depressed for extended periods, you should seek counseling. You may find that all is needed is a simple medication or a conflict resolution through analysis that could mean the difference between misery and sanity.

We are always in a constant state of being. It's about living in the moment and enjoying what we have, today. Not living in a constant state of anxiety and longing for what we must have tomorrow.

Most of all, enjoy the ride. It's the journey, not the destination that's important.

CHAPTER 5

Getting Local Gigs

Clubs

Although clubs represent what is often the most sought after positions for acts, they occupy but a small percentage of available work. Because of the fact that 90% of acts in any given area pursue club work almost exclusively, these jobs are, as a result, the hardest to get and are the lowest paying.

Supply and demand are what drive the economics of any industry, and music is no exception. Club bookers know this and are very selective about what acts they put into their venues. In addition, the pay is also low, since there are many other musicians who are clamoring to get on the stage at the venue, often these jobs pay less than $50–$100 per man for a four hour gig!

The only real advantage booking your act into a club is that, it is a known solid contact for an ongoing source of work and exposure. Unlike private functions such as weddings and parties, which have no specific location or time, other than the one time event and are relatively hard to find, the club offers a venue and a contact for you to hone your marketing efforts to a specific place and person.

The first thing you must determine is whether your act fits the venue. A country group should not be trying to book into a heavy metal club. Visit the club and get the lay of the land. Will your band go over in this place? Is the stage big enough? What kinds of customers patronize the club?

Once you determine a club where your music would be well received, call the club and get the name of the person who books the groups. Get a first and last name, and find out when is the best time to reach them. Be polite and professional, all the time, even if the person on the other end is not.

Now, at this point, I would advise inputting the address, name of the person and phone number, and the best time to reach them into your database program, such as Personal Contact Plus. This way you can schedule the call right on your computer, and keep accurate notes.

Once you get your business of booking your act into high gear, by using this database program, you will have a very organized system for calling, mailing and follow up that will streamline your efforts and will save you many valuable hours of time.

Once you make the call, you will likely get a voice mail to leave a message. Bookers are notoriously difficult to get in touch with, and many of them use voice mail instead of picking up the phone directly. They are badgered constantly by bands trying to get bookings.

Leave a message stating who you are, the name of your group, and that you are interested in booking your group at the club. Tell him that you are sending a press kit, and that you will follow up in two weeks.

Hang up the phone, type into your notes "Left Message, Sent Press Kit" and schedule a follow up call for two weeks out.

Then, put a press kit into an envelope and hit "Print Label" from your database program, and attach the label to your envelope.

Do this with every club you are interested in playing. Get your press kits into the mail at the end of the day, and follow up with each of these contacts in two weeks.

Make once a week follow-up calls until you get the booking.

A word of advice: don't pester the booker, but be persistent. One message a week is plenty. And if you don't get a callback after your fourth week follow up, cease leaving messages and try to see the booker in person to get the final word.

Private Functions

Private events such as parties and wedding receptions are among the best paying jobs. The difficulty in landing them is not knowing when where they are going to take place, since it is usually private individuals who book them.

Contacting rental halls and hotels can be a good strategy, but usually these places are swamped with calls and promo materials from local bands and DJ's, so getting your foot in the door at these places can be hard.

Add to this that many private individuals booking a hall or hotel for a private event also may have their own ideas for entertainment, and it is likely they have hired someone else for the job.

Nonetheless, giving out your cards at private events can lead to referrals for other private events, so always make your cards available and give them out freely, of course. Running ads in the local paper can be cost effective, but not often.

Getting known in your area is a big plus. This is very hard in major markets like Los Angeles, where the metro area is spread out over many miles, and so many acts are competing for work.

This is where a good web site comes in. Web marketing, including good search engine placement on Google is often one of the most effective strategies for landing private work. See our section on websites.

Another place to get the word out are small regional publications that serve specific niche markets. In Los Angeles, we have one called THE JEWISH JOURNAL, where ads are reasonable, and I have heard DJ's and bands get good results in this journal doing Bar Mitzvahs and similar events.

Wedding receptions require a special kind of act, usually a Top 40 cover band that can play wedding reception standards, and who can officiate over the traditional reception activities such as the garter toss, cake cutting and dollar dance.

If you wish to pursue the wedding market and have an act that can handle it, it can be very lucrative.

Check into advertising in one or more of the bridal registry publications, and attend their trade shows. They have mailing lists you can rent. This is hard, expensive marketing, but can pay off if you are not in too tough a market.

If you are going to use mailings to pursue this work, make sure you make it a four color, top-notch presentation. Four color brochure mailings with return cards are the most effective.

One marketing company in Iowa uses pre-printed four color templates that can be customized to your company. They also provide marketing tips for wedding vendors, specializing in Dee-Jays, but the info they provide can also be used for live acts.

Tom Quiner
Breakthrough Marketing
http://www.breakthroughbrochures.com
1-800-810-4152

Caterers

Caterers are always a great source for gigs. The difficulty is that, establishing a relationship where they are getting you jobs can be quite frustrating. Remember, every DJ, band, and party vendor in town is contacting them to solicit work, and usually caterers that are busy are too busy to chat on the phone unless they see a potential upside to it. Caterers are always under deadline, and it seems the many I have contacted are really harried and uptight.

Really, the best way to get in with a caterer is to get them work first. When you book a private party or wedding reception, see if you can't negotiate with your client to hire the catering company you wish to establish relations with.

Handle the negotiations yourself, so that it will be known to the caterer that you are hiring them, not the client. If it is not possible or feasible for you to do this, at least keep your profile high in the referral process: make sure the caterer knows it is you who made this happen, not just an off the cuff referral for your client to call the caterer to mention your name, because chances are, they won't.

If you are sure a catering company in your area gets the kind of jobs that are a fit for your act, put them into your contact database. Make sure they get a call at least once every six months, and that receive something in the mail from you every three months. As always, make sure your marketing materials are stellar.

A good way to break the ice with a catering company is to call them on the phone, introduce yourself, and inquire into their prices. Let them know you are interested in working with them, and that you would be glad to give them referrals if they would be open to the same.

Instead of calling to solicit work, you are calling them to offer them possible work in exchange for consideration of the same. But remember that this can be a stalemate, for if you do not get them work, they will likely not get you work, and the relationship can stall.

But getting yourself known by these companies, you can increase your chances of more referrals.

Event Planners

Event planners are people who organize gatherings for corporate and private organizations, often entailing sales presentations, celebrations, annual meetings, family reunions and such, and handling all phases of the event. This includes staging, lighting, Meals and whatever else is needed for a successful presentation.

Event planners come in all sizes; from a housewife working part-time from home to large national corporations with offices around the world.

They often have a stable of vendors they are familiar with, and they like to stick with them. Often they will work through agents to get entertainment for their functions. Like most people in business, they like to work with people they know and trust. Getting your foot in the door can be tricky.

The methods for marketing yourself to them are the same as with the caterers.

Call them up, and offer to keep them in mind for referral work. Have them send their cards, or better yet, meet with them in person.

Keep them in your contact list, and following the ABC's of marketing and sales: Always Be Closing.

Fundraisers

Fundraising organizations are not often approached by acts because fundraisers are usually not thought of as being a source for gigs. They can be very lucrative.

Fundraisers raise money for all types of organizations and causes; from the local fire department to large concerns like the American Cancer Society, March Of Dimes, American Heart Foundation and thousands more.

Fundraisers make their money by raising money, usually taking a percentage. The vendors they hire such as caterers and musical acts get paid off the top, and usually can get their full fees.

One way to approach fundraisers is to organize a fundraising concert for a charity or cause of their choice. Finding a local celebrity or political figure to Em-Cee the event or appear for a few minutes on stage can add greatly to the prestige factor of the event, and can give you a lot of clout with the fundraiser.

Finding fundraisers is as close as your local yellow pages, listed under same.

Also check "charitable organizations," and keep an eye on your local newspaper for people active in fundraising. Usually the society pages cover fundraising dinners and list the names of the chairmen in the article. Look their numbers up and pitch them on your act, letting them know you would like to get behind their cause.

Non-profit organizations do not mean "No profit" for the vendors who help these orgs raise money, and if you connect with enough of these, you can keep your calendar booked solid all year. It will take time to build, but will be worth your time.

Country Clubs

Most country clubs have banquet facilities, and is usually overseen by a banquet manager or director of catering, an in-house position which puts them in direct contact with clients wishing to rent the facility for special events.

Many of these events are wedding receptions, but can also include political functions, awards dinners, rotary club meetings and other local gatherings. Many of these events require entertainment, and that's where you come in.

John McCullough of Liberty Music in Philadelphia, provides soloists such as pianists and small combos for special events, and has found success in booking country clubs. John (See interview section) works the country clubs in his area this way:

"Get a listing of all the golf courses and country clubs within your travel area, and go down the list, calling the main desk and ask who their banquet manager is, and their direct line or extension. Usually you get a voice mailbox when you call the banquet manager."

"Leave a message introducing yourself, your company, and the types of music you provide. Let them know you are mailing them some cards and brochures. Send out your materials right away. Follow up two weeks after you've sent the materials, and then follow up once every three months with both a mailing and a phone call."

"It takes time and hard work to build a clientele, it took me three years before I got anything steady out of them. But I am working on other things while building it up. You get a little from here a little from there and when you get enough of those built up, it adds up to year round work."

Casinos

Depending on your geographic location, casinos may be an option for you to consider. Many states are legalizing gambling, and in some parts of the country, Indian Gaming Casinos are becoming increasingly prevalent.

With a casino, you are facing the same sort of competition and mindset you are dealing with the clubs. A casino offers two areas for a musician to work: lounge or showroom.

Showroom acts are usually name acts called "hard tickets," and are limited to the larger "stars." It is sometimes possible to sell a tribute act into a showroom, but it's gotten more difficult in a tightening economy.

In Las Vegas and Atlantic City, the use of "canned music" or pre-recorded tracks for backing music has become more common, creating less jobs for musicians.

Lounges are set up for one thing: to get the customer in for a drink or two and get him back out onto the gaming floor to spend money. This is why many casinos don't book showroom style acts into the lounges.

Lounge acts generally play 5–6 sets per night consisting mostly of covers and Top 40. It's a tough gig, the hours are long and the pay usually isn't tremendous. If you can land a lounge act spot and work 5–6 nights per week, you can earn $1000 a week per man, sometimes more, sometimes less.

This can make the difference between trying to seak out a living doing weekend gigs while trying to hold down a 9–5 job, and working as a full time musician in a lounge, where you will be employed on a steady basis, even if the contract is only three months.

Casino Lounge work is a grind; the burnout rate is high, and it can really stall a career if an act has aspirations for a showroom gig.

The advantage to lounge work is it's steady, provides good exposure, and the money is adequate to make a living from. Being a full-time performer can be a great feeling.

It also has its drawbacks. Some performers don't do well in a casino environment. They fall pray to social ills like alcoholism, gambling, smoking, and other unhealthy vices.

If you can use your free time wisely, reading, working out, pursuing healthy activities, staying off the gaming tables and away from the bottle, stay focused, healthy and in control of your career, a casino gig might be the ideal job for you.

But know going in that it requires a lot of self-discipline to keep it a growth situation and not denigrate into a nightmare world of depression, booze, and gambling.

Churches

Often, churches have plenty of talent from within their congregations willing to work for free for various church functions. But active churches often have special events through the year, such as bake sales, fundraisers, dances and other get-togethers requiring live music.

The best way to keep up with these events is to get on every church mailing list you can find. Most churches have a monthly newsletter they send out via regular or email.

When these church bulletins arrive, scan them for upcoming activities. When you see an event that could benefit from live music, contact the church and find out who you can talk to pitch your services.

You can also approach them and offer to do a concert fundraiser to help raise money for their organization. You would make your money off the top in such an arrangement, and can also take a percentage of the ticket price.

Schools

Schools are a great source for gigs. These are broken down into the subcategories: Elementary, High and Colleges.

Elementary Schools

These schools hire performers to do assemblies, and the acts they hire offer entertainment that has some sort of educational angle to the program. Developing an act that is both educational and entertaining and can hold the attention of kids is a challenging job, but the rewards are great.

First of all, you are doing something good for children. Secondly, the money is great: An established performer doing a solo act can command as high as $1000 per 45 minute show!

Marketing your act to the schools is a matter of purchasing a mailing list from the department of education and sending them flyers and prices on your show, and showing the benefits to their children.

This is a market where referrals really count. It's not an easy market to crack, and schools tend to hire only performers they have seen before, often at other schools.

Before attempting to go after this market, I would recommend reading the best book out there on this subject:

How to Make Money Performing in Schools: The Definitive Guide to Developing, Marketing, and Presenting School Assembly Programs
by *David Heflick*

High Schools

High Schools aren't a goldmine for musicians wishing to find gigs, as high schools have enough young musicians with a local following who will play most of the high school functions for free or very little money. High school dances are the most common functions hired out, however, there are often graduation parties which occur each June for the outgoing senior grads, and these graduation parties often have a theme.

Contact the high school and ask them who is organizing their senior graduation functions, preferably a member of the faculty who is overseeing any student who may be working on the committee. You will find faculty members will be the easiest to reach, but you are still going to be leaving messages.

Introduce yourself and your services and ask if you might be able to put together an entertainment package for the graduation that would reflect the theme they are planning.

Colleges

Colleges are one of the greatest sources of wonderful paying gigs for entertainers, and, as a result, this market is the toughest to crack. There are about 2800 colleges in the U.S. that constantly hire entertainment.

Colleges often have big budgets and hire entertainers who travel all over the United States, playing "The Circuit."

This circuit is largely controlled by NACA, the National Association For Campus Activities. There are a stable of booking agencies that serve this market exclusively, and those agencies are highly selective whom they represent.

Each year, NACA holds a conference that showcases artists wishing to land college gigs, and getting a spot in the showcases can be a tricky and expensive proposition.

To become a member of NACA is $583 per year, and is necessary to be considered for a showcase, unless you have an agent who is a NACA member agent, then he can submit you for showcases under his "umbrella."

The simplest way to get your foot in the door on the college circuit is to find an influential college booking agent to take you on as a client, representing you to NACA. This is not an easy task at all, but it's the least expensive option.

If you can't find an agent to represent you, you have no choice but to go it alone. This involves having flyers printed about your act, your prices, renting a mailing list, and sending out mailings at least once a year. You will also need a video and a promo kit to send out to the colleges who respond to your mailing.

The biggest drawback to booking colleges is the expense of travel and routing. If you can book a "tour" of colleges that is intelligently routed, you can make a nice chunk of money, but it's really only the bigger agents that the clout to book you on such a tour.

Unless you have an act that does really well at a showcase, or is in great demand, then you will be forced to hopscotch all over the country playing gigs that are hundreds of miles apart, and this can eat up your profits quickly.

I approached the college market as a solo artist singer-songwriter, playing a mixed bag of college and party standards and contemporary folk-rock. I was unable to land an agent, so went forward with renting a mailing list and sending out two major mailings of around 1000 flyers each. My Unique Selling Proposition was price; because I knew I was not in demand and was a solo artist (the dreaded WSS, white singer-songwriter, in college booking parlance, a very common animal), my pitch was that I could "Rock Your Crowd, Not Your Budget."

My price was $450 per one hour gig, which included travel. My plan was to book at least one other gig or school within driving distance of the primary college gig, therefore doubling my income without incurring extra plane fare.

Out of 2000 pieces, I got about 10 requests for videos, and out of those, 4 gig offers. Problem is, those gig offers were in Wyoming, Florida, and Pennsylvania, and were not during the same months.

I booked the Wyoming gig and immediately contacted all the colleges within driving distance with no success at procuring other bookings during that particular two day period. I tried contacting clubs but none of them were hiring singer-songwriters, so in the end, I had to cancel the gig.

Ultimately, I did not take these gig offers because my plane fare and car rental would eat up all my profits. By the time I added up my mailing, printing and promotional materials, I ended up losing several thousand dollars going after the colleges.

I tried going out again by doubling my price, but then I placed myself in the same price range as many other unknown WSS's, and therefore killed my USP.

In the end, I gave up on colleges. Or my own particular situation, they did not work for me. But if you are a comic, solo artist, or have an act that would appeal to the college market, and you are free to travel, you might want to try this market out.

It can pay off in the long run, if you stick with it, but add up your numbers carefully. The expense of marketing and travel can eat up all your profits, fast.

Better to land an agent for this market and let them handle the marketing expense, and route you intelligently so you are not spending needless time and dollars on hopscotch travel.

A very good source for information on breaking into this market and a great college mailing list is:

Breaking Into The College Market   *http://www.cdbaby.net/derek/college.htm*

Hotels

See "road gigs-domestic."

House Concerts

One form of gigging that has gained popularity in the last two years is house concerts. A person will open their living room to a live presentation and charge $10 per person to attend, and give the funds to the performer.

There are many variations on this theme, but the upshot is that you can make $100 per gig or more by the time the monies are collected, and these gigs are great for selling merchandise, especially CD's.

Audiences are small and appreciative, and the intimacy playing in a home environment is hard to beat.

House concerts are held in many major cities and small towns. Look up House Concerts and type your city or location into Google and see what comes up. There are also many websites which feature an overview and listings of house concerts, and how to organize them.

Can't find a house concert to play at? Put on your own. All you need is a living room and someone who is willing to host it. But keep in mind that promoting shows successfully is a difficult road. Getting butts in seats is never easy.

Once you build a following, it can pay off.

Fairs

Fairs are held in every county across America. They consist of a main stage and usually one or more side stages. The main stage slots are for name or established groups with a 45–60 minute show. The side stages are reserved for local acts and singer-songwriters, whose performance lengths can range from one set to five sets, depending on the needs of the fair organizers.

The best way to book fairs is through an agent, or contact the office of the fair directly. They will, of course, ask you to send your promo materials, and usually at least six months in advance.

Competition is keen for the paying slots. Side stage slots usually do not pay a great deal, and can vary greatly in their compensation. Sometimes an act will play these stages for free, simply to sell their merchandise, but beware this is a tough road to riches.

The average pay for a main stage slot is $1500–$2500 for a five piece group.

To locate fairs in your area, and learn more about them, check out: *http://www.fairsnet.org*

Festivals

Did you know there are thousands of festivals held every year, and many opportunities in your local area to play them? It's true. Festivals are generally held in the Spring, Summer and Fall and have a theme.

Many times the themes revolve around specific kinds of food—such as strawberries, onions, garlic—you name it. Festival organizers like to book local groups that can play a variety of music, or play to a theme.

For instance, in Long Beach, California the local festival is a beach theme, and surf music and Beach Boy Tributes are quite popular.

Festivals require a lot of tedious calling, mailing and follow up, so you would do well to scan your local papers and the internet for any festivals being advertised, and contact them to get their mailing and contact info for next year.

By the time you see their ads, it will likely mean they have booked their entertainment for this year. Put them into your database and schedule a mailing and phone call to get a jump on the following year.

Early birds get the worm in this game, and by careful and diligent follow up and a decent presentation, you could have an annual gig.

Feeder Gigs—Playing Free To Get Paying Jobs— The Power Of "FREE" and how viral marketing can fill your calendar—if you can take it!

Play for free? Many musicians shudder at the thought. But there are times when playing a gig for free can pay you more than if you blew the gig off. Why? Because certain gigs give you exposure to your target market.

Many times competition is such that your act will never get its foot in the door. Playing for free is one way to overcome this problem; few bookers will turn down an offer for you to play for free.

But you must bargain with some leverage. By selling your act out for free, you place a price tag on your value. This is the biggest disadvantage to playing free.

But if you do this in the act of helping others, say perhaps for a charitable event, you can expose yourself to the kinds of people that will pay you to play future gigs. It's a slippery slope, to be sure, but if you can be convinced that you can reasonably expect to get paying gigs from your free performance, it's worth a try, especially when trying to break a new act.

The key here is to use 'viral marketing" when you play. Make sure the booker or promoter agrees you can give out flyers and conduct a raffle to give away a prize, in which the collection of names for your mailing list is a requirement.

When I was just getting started with my act, I went online and emailed every chamber of commerce I could find within driving distance, offering to play a free show to get exposure.

Several months later I was contacted by a realtor who was a member of one chamber and he hired me to play a show for $50. That one show has resulted in paid sponsorships for my concerts as well as other paying gigs from the chamber.

You want every person that sees you to tell another person about you, hence the term "viral marketing."

By conducting a "door prize" drawing, in which each person fills out a small card or slip of paper with blanks for with their name, address, and email, you will be able to collect a sizeable mailing list to use for future gigs.

If you continue to do this, collecting mailing list names and playing "feeder" gigs where large numbers of influential people will see you, you will develop a following and paying gigs will come. It takes time, patience, and perseverance, but it works, if you work it.

CHAPTER 6

Making Your Own Local Gigs

This chapter concerns creating your own gigs, and describes a number of ways you can "DIY," or "Do It Yourself." Many of the traditional venues and methods for getting gigs are jammed with competition that it's often very difficult to make any headway, particularly in a crowded market.

The solution to this is to create gigs where none existed before, thus being the only act that will do the gig. Here are some ways I have found useful. Feel free to invent some of your own.

Four Walling/Two Walling—Your Act In Concert

A fairly new business model has emerged from the new economy. "Four-walling" and "Two-walling" venues. This involves renting or co-renting a club, space, or theater and doing the advertising and promoting yourself, as well as ticket sales. You take all or part of the ticket money, depending on your arrangement with the venue.

One extreme example of this is in Las Vegas. Almost all showroom performers rent the casino showroom, either with their own production companies or in partnership with a producing entity. Sometimes they are partners with the casino, sometimes not. (See the Chapter on "Making It In Las Vegas" for more on this.)

But for our purposes here, we are talking about your going to a venue on your own in your community and renting out the facility with your own money.

This can be great for an act with a great draw, but disastrous if people don't show up. The public is fickle, and one can never predict in what numbers they may turn out to see an event. Many is a concert promoter who has gone into bankruptcy this way.

I have had some successes "Four-walling" my Elvis Tribute Show and other tribute acts into small theaters. It's a high risk gamble, and if you can't afford to roll the dice, don't do it. I have friends who have made money producing tribute shows and even name acts into theaters, but even they will tell you that sometimes they lose as much as they win.

As a Producer/Promoter, you are responsible for everything. You would be amazed how many details go into producing even the smallest show. There are contracts to sign, insurance policies, printing, and advertising and promotion tasks. There are an endless number of jobs that must be performed to an exact timetable. Screw up on any of them, you could lose your shirt.

But when it goes well, it *can* go *very well.* Let's say you rent a 1000-seat venue for $3000, plus $1000 for the house sound and lights and stage personnel. Add in another $1000 for box office services and miscellaneous things like insurance and catering, you are in for $5000. Add to this your advertising costs of say, $2000, and another $2000 for your band and opening act.

So now you are in for about $10,000, as an example. If you sell your tickets for even $20, that's a 10,000 profit!

But you must factor in the many weeks of prep it takes to produce and promote the show, and that you must sell every seat to make that kind of profit. At half capacity, you've only broken even.

Believe me, it's no fun putting months of work and $10,000 of your own money into a show and have a bad turnout. If you are performing on top of that you are in the unfortunate position of having to work your ass off, perform, and still lose money!

Remember, this can go the other way. It's a great feeling selling out a show and walking away with decent profit, and in the process be able to play on a large stage to an appreciative concert audience.

There are so many factors and variables that can affect the turnout greatly: Is it a weeknight (less than ideal) or a Saturday (ideal). Is it a holiday weekend, is it raining/snowing that night?

Is the economy in a downward cycle? Are we in a war with yet another foreign country? Are you under pricing or overpricing your tickets? Is the theater well-trafficked and have they had your flyers in the lobby for sufficient enough time as to attract patrons attending their other shows? Have they included you in their season mailer, even if they aren't presenting your show as part of their season?

The public is so sensitive to these issues it can prevent them from venturing out of their cocoons for any kind of event. Add to this that there are many choices for people to spend their time off and their entertainment dollars.

Even staying at home can be far preferable to going out and enduring traffic, crowds, and a potentially bad show. With home theater and gaming systems in almost every home, plus internet and other distractions, you can see that getting people to go out to your show can become a difficult task at best.

But, let's say you are a single acoustic performer with a large following. Since you have no costs for a band, you can take the ticket money for yourself. If you book a smaller venue of 500 seats and still charge $20, you could walk away with a tidy profit, since the cost of the theater rental is less for a smaller venue and you wouldn't be paying a backup band.

To offset your risk, you might consider "two walling" with the venue, meaning you split the profit/loss equally with the venue. If it's a theater, you simply split rent and ticket money. If it's a club, you might consider taking the door ticket money while the club gets the drinks and food.

This way you can see what your turnout will be and then maybe take your act to a nearby town and try four-walling another venue yourself.

You will find smaller theaters are more willing to help you than larger ones. In fact, in Los Angeles, many of the larger theaters have a strict policy to NOT help you promote.

They are committed to promoting their own season shows, and often feel that to help fledgling promoters pulls their focus away from their own projects. But also be aware that many smaller theaters have little staff and can rarely afford someone to help you market your show.

If your act has a major following or some pre-sold elements (as in a tribute act) and you think you can fill those seats, you just might have the perfect situation for a successful four-wall. But proceed with caution, this is an area where you can lose money in a hurry!

If you do decide to four-wall a small theater, make sure

- Start early; six–twelve months is a nice window
- The theater is well attended by patrons throughout the year, so they will see your flyers in the lobby
- The theater is at least somewhat open to helping you market your show
- You get a Saturday night for your show, not a weeknight
- You do a prize drawing to get your audience to join your mailing list
- You have theater include you in their season mailing
- To have theater include you in their newspaper advertising
- To promote your show using flyers, email, and posters
- You start promoting at least 3 months in advance of date
- To try to find local businesses to sponsor your show to offset cost

Finding sponsors to contribute to your show in exchange for an ad in your program can often make the difference between loss and profit. But finding sponsors is a tough, time consuming job, and can become a very difficult pursuit on top of your other duties.

You may be able to find someone within your sphere of influence to make phone calls to local business on your behalf to solicit donations in exchange for a percentage.

Four walling can be a very satisfying way to build your audience and make a profit. It offers a great way to get your name out to the local community, and allows you to sell your merchandise after the show.

Make sure you have some money put aside so you can four wall a number of theaters in different regions, within driving distance or one overnight stay. As these shows become more successful, you can schedule them as an annual concert, while expanding your circle around your home base radius.

For a detailed look at one man's odyssey into producing a highly successful concert from scratch, obtain a copy of:

The Concert Book—James Hollon

Clubs

As mentioned before, clubs and bars are tough places to get gigs, and even then it's harder still to walk away with anything other than some pocket change for some long hours. Add to this the fact that clubs are the places where all the other acts are trying to get work, your chances for success are next to nil. Screw that!

Approach a club that can seat at least 500 people and tell them you'll bring in your following and work for ticket money or "the door", if they will agree to make their money from drinks and food. Split the advertising cost with the club, and try to get a guarantee.

You probably won't get the guarantee and you might lose money if you don't draw, but if you have a decent size mailing list and are confident you can bring in the bodies, you may make out quite well.

If you got even 300 people in the door at $10 per person, that's $3000, minus advertising and mailing expenses, which can be split with the club. Not a huge profit if you have a five piece band, but it's better than the $50–$100 per man you'll get trying to get the club owner to pay the band straight out.

Now, keep in mind this is not the best way to make money doing gigs; I consider it to be a last resort, but sometimes it's a great way to fill out your calendar. One good thing about clubs is that there are plenty of them, so if you had one of these a month it would be a decent form of profit and exposure, just keep in mind it's a limited one.

Theaters

We've already covered four-walling theaters, but I want to mention also that many theaters have regular seasons where they hire acts to come in and do their shows to fill out their dramatic schedules.

Community and fine-arts theaters usually put on musicals and stage plays during their seasons, selling tickets to their subscribers. Pitch them on the idea of hiring your act to fill out their season, and you may have a paying gig that turns out to be an annual event.

Busking

Here is an interesting area of gigging not often covered, and that is "busking," or playing on the street for tips. Sounds like begging? Well, in a way it is, but it's a time honored tradition and one not to be overlooked. Although more popular in Europe than in America, busking can be profitable, and just plain grass-roots fun.

Buskers are generally acoustic performers who set up and play in crowded areas such as subways, train stations, outside of concert halls, busy sections of business districts, anywhere they know there will be a crowd.

Playing their instruments with a bucket at their feet, or passing the hat, singing and jiving and attracting attention, these musicians are carrying on the minstrel tradition in modern times.

Buskers aren't getting rich; sometimes several hours of busking results in a hundred dollars in tips, sometimes more, often-times less.

But there is a freedom in busking, a true pioneer spirit that can be exhilarating as well as liberating.

Before considering busking, you would do well to check your local city ordinance and see if a vendor's license is required to solicit donations by playing music in a public place.

Sometimes it's as simple as buying a $50 license. In other areas, you will find no laws pertaining to it. In most cases, you likely will not be bothered by authorities.

Know your rights going in.

Success in busking is all about location, location, and then location.

The idea is to attract a dense crowd, draw them into your "stage area", which can be as simple as a small rope sectioning off a plywood crate ("applebox"). You as the performer need to get "above" the crowd.

The more flamboyant your appearance, the more attention you will attract. One example of this are traditional folk music performers dressing in Medieval costumes. Jugglers and fire-eaters make quite a spectacle, and while I don't propose you shoot fire into the air, you get the general idea that the more people you attract, the more money you'll make.

And on this subject, it is important you solicit PAPER MONEY, not CHANGE! If you ask for change, you will get change. Drop a few Lincolns into your hat so the people get the right idea!

Busking is not for everyone. You can spend a lot of time in less than favorable conditions, but if you slant the odds in your favor, this can be a rewarding and satisfying experience.

With the right location and a little creativity, you may be able to set up a busking situation that is both profitable and fun.

Churches

A great source of gigs, churches are often overlooked by musicians. The greatest thing about churches is that there are so many of them. The feature that I like best about churches is that usually, there is a church office that is open 9–5 on weekdays, and friendly people will usually answer the phone.

The first source of a gig at a church is to join their house band for the Sunday service. This is normally not a well-paying position, but its something. The second way is to contact the church and convince them to allow you to put on a concert at their church for which you can sell tickets.

This involves a little legwork and promotion on your part, but the basic idea is to have the church get behind your concert by announcing your show to their congregation every Sunday during their services and in their church newsletter and website.

If you offer to split the money from ticket sales with the church, you will usually find a willing reception, but remember there is still two factors of risk: the first is getting the church to go along with your idea, and the second is selling enough tickets to make it worth your while to tie up a prime gig night doing the concert.

My own experience with this is that it generally takes a lot of phone calling and follow up to get a church to consider your idea, and further legwork of meeting them to explain your plan in person. You need to be clean, articulate and able to meet skepticism head on. Often the church will ask to see a demo, and there is also the matter of the type of music being "appropriate" for a church gathering.

Sometimes just good music is good enough to pass this test, other times a church that is more fundamental in its leanings may want spiritual or gospel type music as the concert basis.

If your church concert is well attended and you get good reports from the church elders, this can easily turn into an annual event.

A good place to start is the internet. There are a lot of church website search engines where you can type in your zip code and get listings of churches in your area. Print them out and start calling.

Generally, you will be leaving messages for the pastor of the church, and generally your call won't be returned, especially if they think you are trying to sell them something. Since they don't know you, they will assume you are doing just that, but don't be deterred.

Churches like shows that are family oriented, so wholesome themes work, such as "Sock Hop 50's Show," "Hawaiian Luau," etc.

Keep the kind of music you would like to do pretty general, like "oldies rock and roll," or "Spiritual," and stay away from hard rock and roll and rap, unless the church caters to this type of music lover.

There are many different types of churches and denominations. You will begin to pick up patterns as to which churches are most open to your concerts, and once you establish yourself at one church, you will find others in the same family of churches will be more open to your playing at their venues.

You may even be able to set up a "circuit" where your act can travel full time, or simply get enough work locally to keep your calendar filled all year long.

Hospitals

Here is another gig source that is overlooked by musicians. Hospitals hold events through the year, much like many large companies, such as Christmas Parties and annual fundraisers. They also hold award dinners to honor various employees such as doctors and administrators.

Call the hospital and ask who handles their entertainment for special events.

Creating your own gig at a hospital is the same as for churches. Many non-profit hospitals have foundations who administrate the fundraising and management of the non-profit hospital. By calling a hospital, asking if they are non-profit, and then upon hearing so, ask for the number of the foundation for the hospital, you can call this foundation and offer your services to do a fundraising concert.

Large hospitals can attract large crowds just from their employee and donor bases, and they often have large public relations departments that can publicize the event, often garnering lots of local press.

I worked briefly for a large hospital PR department and was astounded by the streamlined business they had built publicizing special events that were designed to be fundraisers.

Hospitals are always on the lookout for ways to get themselves into print that will give them a positive profile in their local communities, because this equates to money in the form of donations by wealthy members of their communities.

Getting "in" at a hospital foundation requires tact, perseverance, and diligent follow up. Once you are "in" and one hospital, you can use your success as a springboard to attract other hospitals.

With hospitals as well as any other fundraising, garner as much press as you can on your successful fundraising efforts, and use copies of these articles to include in your press kit and on your website.

Business Concerts

This technique was pioneered by Jana Stansfield, a singer-songwriter with a few good books of her own. Basically, it involves contacting a company or business that has at least 100 employees and offering to do a free after-work or lunch concert in their lunchroom.

This is great for weeknights or weekdays when you would normally not have a gig, and using this method, you would "pass the can" for tips and donations and sell your CD's. For a one hour gig at a fairly decent size company, you can make at least $150–$300, even more, and the people are appreciative. Often these same companies will hire you for their company Christmas Party or other such event, and the individual workers will also be a good source for private work.

"Passing The Can" works better when you have a volunteer walking the can from person to person and encouraging donations. When I say "can," I mean a large coffee can that has colored paper wrapped around it and either printed on or magic markered "DONATIONS."

Cut an opening in the plastic lid allowing people to slip their folded bills into the can. Tell the people "no coins, folks, bills only, and make sure they are of a respectable denomination."

You should announce at some point during your show that you are going to send the can around for donations, and encourage the people to "be generous, for the wealth you share today will be your reward tomorrow. We are especially fond of Abraham Lincoln and Alexander Hamilton, but if you could find it in your hearts to include a few Andrew Jacksons, we would be forever grateful and you have just made a generous contribution to the arts in your community."

Remember you must *ask* for donations, people need to be motivated to dig deep, and if someone from their company is walking the can around, they will feel that much more obligated to give.

Make sure you have plenty of CD's on display, and any other merchandise you may have available such as t-shirts and photos. When people like your show, they want to buy souvenirs, make them readily available and announce their availability during your show.

Timing is also to be kept in mind, paydays are the ideal time for these types of shows.

Follow up with the company principals every three months or so to see if you can return, or if there are any events which the company would like you to perform at for a fee.

CHAPTER 7

Road Gigs—Domestic

Hotels

There was a time when hotels had lounges and those lounges hired entertainment six nights a week. Often these gigs employed road groups who traveled "circuits" and were a great source of gigs for many musicians. That situation eroded in the late 80's, but there are still many hotel lounges that hire acts for weekends. These gigs usually don't pay a whole lot, involve 4–5 sets a night, and are tough to get.

That being said, if your act includes Top 40 and you can keep your ensemble small, there are still opportunities out there. You won't make a whole helluva lot of money, but you can gain valuable experience.

Booking a gig at these hotels involves getting hotel guides and listings that indicate which hotels have entertainment.

Holiday Inn publishes a free guide available at any Intercontinental, Crowne-Plaza, Holiday Inn/Express, Staybridge or Priority Club location. Under each listing, it indicates which hotels have live entertainment. Online, go to: *http://www.6c.com*

The second area hotels can provide road gigs domestically is for private parties and events held at the hotel. These events come in through the Banquet and Catering department, and are just about impossible to land, and even harder to get while on the road.

In order to network for these jobs, you must contact each hotel and ask for the Banquet and Catering manager, then speak with that person about your act. You will be given the usual "send your stuff" routine, and your package will likely go promptly ignored. But it's worth a try if you can follow up on your package and think you would enjoy this type of performing, and you can make the money work.

If you are good at follow up, this method can yield good results, but if you can't do the follow up, don't bother. The contacts for these gigs are busy, and they won't often call you. You have to be the aggressor and call them.

The third source of gigs domestically at the hotels are at the "higher class" hotels, such as the Ritz-Carlton. They will often employ soloists such as pianists or harp players in their lobbies or restaurants.

These positions are handled by the banquet and catering departments of the hotels, and you will sometimes be referred to an outside agent who handles the bookings.

If you are working a soloist gig at a hotel, either while traveling or locally, steer clear of the gossip and politics of the hotel and be professional to the hilt. Do not drink or smoke, and never swear. Hotels will fire you in an instant if they think you do not represent their name in a respectable manner.

Clubs

Booking clubs for a tour uses the same strategy as working clubs locally: phone calls and follow ups. You'll have to do some research on what clubs are in the areas you'll be touring through, and the dates you want the gigs for. You may have an advantage over local bands in the area because you will be perceived as more professional because you are on a tour, hence you may be given more consideration by the club booker.

Dinner Theaters

If your act lends itself to a more cabaret style of music, dinner theaters can be a great source for work. Dinner theaters exist in almost every large town, and often the people who manage them are friendly and family oriented.

These places tend to run musicals and murder-mystery type of shows, but if you have a unique act that is family oriented and entertaining, this might be a great way to go. I have a friend who is a Frank Sinatra impersonator, and he does well on this circuit.

Bars

Don't overlook bars while planning your tour: most can't pay much but they might be a good staple as fill-ins around your tent pole gigs. It's tougher to contact these places and get anyone on the phone who can help you, but there is usually someone there who can tell you who the contact is and when they will be in.

If you are a single act, you might consider passing the can at these places, you can make several hundred dollars an evening if the place is crowded enough.

House Concerts

There are house concerts held all across the nation, and all you need to do to be considered for a booking at them is consult websites which show listings of them, and call the house owners who host them. Let them know you are planning a tour and would like to make their house concert a stop along the way.

Casinos

Casinos don't generally book one nighters or touring road acts unless the acts have a name. However, the lounges located within the casinos sometimes consider acts that tour. Use the same methods for contact as outlined in the former chapter on Casinos.

CHAPTER 8

Road Gigs—Overseas

Hotels and Resorts

Want to travel out of the country? There are lots of hotels and resorts overseas, and with a little persistence, you can be working them. Usually these venues are booked by booking agents located in the country where the venues are located, but some US based agents will sometimes handle them.

Generally resorts book their acts for three month terms, but there are many exceptions to this rule.

The best way to get these gigs is to call the hotel and ask for the banquet or catering manager, or the person who handles the entertainment booking for the hotel. Many of these contacts will speak English, but if they don't, ask for someone at the front desk who does.

Cruise Ships

Please see our chapter on cruise ships.

CHAPTER 9

Making It In Las Vegas

Want To Make It In Las Vegas? Read This First!

At some point or another, many performers dream of moving to Las Vegas to make it as an entertainer. While it's true that many opportunities abound in this show business capital, it's also true that its one of the roughest places in the world to succeed in.

The advantage to Las Vegas is that it's where the most work is. With the many casinos, and each of them hiring entertainment in their showrooms and lounges, it's a buffet of opportunity.

The cost of living is reasonable, the climate, although warm, is dry and sunny. There's a ton of work, and it's an exciting, twenty-four hour town. It's also a place where a performer can go from waiting tables to starring in a multimillion dollar production show almost overnight.

So why is Las Vegas so difficult for many to "break into?"

The reasons for this are many. Competition for gigs in Las Vegas is very intense, because there are so many musicians living there that are competing for the same jobs. So if you are a top 40 band or musician, you will be fighting with hundreds of other musicians seeking the same jobs.

If you are a performer such as a singer, and want to get work in the many showrooms in the city, you will run into a fairly new phenomenon that has taken place in Vegas, and that is the practice of "Four-walling."

Many of the big acts playing the showrooms of Las Vegas are backed by large entertainment investment companies who actually rent the showrooms for extended periods. All advertising and expenses related to the show are paid for by the investment company, who in turn collects the money for the tickets.

So, if you think you may be the next great singer, performer, magician, illusionist or whatever, you will need a lot of money in the form of investors to try to get your foothold in the Las Vegas showroom market.

"Some showrooms are empty during the day, and you can sometimes work a deal with the entertainment director of the casino to two or four wall the showroom for a day show," reveals Robbie Howard, a fifteen year veteran of the Las Vegas gigging circuit. (See interview.)

Howard has made a decent living from two-walling showrooms for day shows, collecting only a small drink fee from each patron, who must buy the minimum drink ticket for admission to an otherwise free show.

MAKING IT IN LAS VEGAS

Casinos hire lounge acts, this is true, and usually these bookings are handled by the entertainment directors at each casino. There are also agents based in Las Vegas who have influence over the ED's who handle the rooms. All of the casinos have at least one person who handles entertainment, a call to each hotel will yield you the name and contact info of the person you need to speak to.

You must be very persistent but not make a pest of yourself with these contacts. They are very busy people, but they are often fair and good business people, unlike many of the club bookers, who can be gruff and arrogant.

Call them up and introduce yourself and briefly describe your act. If you get a voice mail, do the same. Ask them if they would be interested in an act like yours. If you get a callback to send it, do so. If you've reached him or her directly, and they say send it, go for it.

Your package should include a personalized cover letter, a video, photo, bio and press clips.

Send it and follow up two weeks later. Don't get angry with them if they haven't looked at your stuff. Keep calling every two weeks until you get a response. Offer to go audition your act for free.

It's all about luck and timing, and a lot of persistence to get the gig. As always, bookers are insanely busy people. You have to make a lot of noise to get their attention, but you must never be gruff or unprofessional with them or you will lose any chance of ever dealing with them again.

Be nice, courteous, professional, and diligent. Don't be a pest.

Las Vegas is sometimes considered a tough town, the climate is dry and can wreak havoc on your singing voice (a phenomenon known as "Vegas Throat"). The summers are extremely hot, and socially speaking, it's not a warm and fuzzy place to hang out in. But if you are tough skinned and persistent, then go there and network.

Working in a casino is also not the healthiest of environments. There are a lot of chronic gamblers, drinkers and smokers, and the cigarette smoke creates health hazards in the form of upper respiratory infections and lung cancer. Smoke can also adversely affect your vocal cords.

If braving the rigors of the casino trade wins out against the prospect of dying a slow death in small town America, and you are ready to soldier up the hill and take the fort, go in well-armed and with a strategy.

Don't send your package to everybody who requests it unless you feel they are a good fit for your act. Remember that most agents are going to want to see your package whether or not they can book you or not. Sometimes, they will tell you to send your package just to get you off the phone.

A good strategy with these agents is to send them an "InfoFax," a short three page document that contains a description of your act, a small photo, a bio, and possibly a press clip or review. In very large letters on this document, place a link to your website and indicate your video and audio clips, as well as other pertinent data, are available at your website.

Have them preview your materials on your website first. If they feel you have something they can book, then send them the package.

Get to know the people who book the hotels, and contact every agent you can find that may be a fit for your act.

As always, keep both an index card file and a computer database and work it daily. By staying in front of the people who book the acts, you increase your chances ten fold of booking the gigs. Schedule a phone call to each contact at least once a month to every two weeks. Any more than this and you may be considered a pest.

Sandy Hackett, another veteran performer in Las Vegas, has made a full time living as a comedian and performer. (See interview.) His advice is to "audition for everything, knock on a lot of doors and believe in yourself. Nobody ever got booked sitting at home."

If you do get the gig, stay away from the gaming tables. More than a few Las Vegas entertainers found their way on the road to ruin with their gambling habits, and many of their problems started at that innocent looking slot machine.

Las Vegas Resources:

CALLBACK MAGAZINE
2375 E. Tropicana
Ste. #6, Las Vegas. NV 89119
702/891-9222;
www.callbacknews.com

LAS VEGAS ENTERTAINERS
www.lasvegasentertainers.com

LV AUDITIONS
www.lvauditions.com
Community theater auditions

SHOW BIZ WEEKLY
702/990-2463

VEGAS AUDITIONS
www.vegasauditions.com

CHAPTER 10

Cruise Ships

Market Overview
Types Of Gigs and What They Pay
How and Who To Contact
What They Look For

Getting Cruise Ship Gigs

Market Overview

So you want to travel the world, see exotic ports, meet new people in new cultures, and make money playing music in the process? A cruise ship gig might be just the thing for you.

Cruise ships represent one of the fastest growing segments of the live music industry.

Today there are over 25 major cruise lines, and almost all of them hire some form of live music. Of the 100+ ships in the cruise market, many hundreds of jobs are available to musicians. Norwegian Cruise Lines boasts they have over 200 positions filled at any given time for full-time musicians!

At this writing, the major cruise lines are:

American Cruise Lines
Bora Bora Cruises
Carnival Cruise Lines
Celebrity Cruises
Costa Cruises
Crystal Cruises
Cunard Line
Disney Cruise Line
First European Cruises
Fred. Olsen Cruise Lines
Holland America Line
MSC Italian Cruises
Norwegian Coastal Voyages
Norwegian Cruise Lines
Oceania Cruises*
Orient Cruises
Princess Cruises
Radisson Seven Seas Cruise Line
Regal Cruises**
Royal Caribbean International
Royal Olympia Cruises
Seabourn Cruise Line
Silversea Cruises
Swan Hellenic*
Windstar Cruises

(See index for complete address and phone numbers).

Although a cruise ship gig can be a great experience, they are not for everyone.

First of all is the challenge of *getting* the gig. Competition is fierce for musician positions on the ships, simply because so many musicians think it's a paradise job. (It can be for some, but often isn't.) The upside is that there is a fair amount of turnover, so if you have the talent, a professional looking package and are persistent, you'll probably land a gig.

Most cruise ships hire for positions in their house band or orchestra, and usually require that you read music. The house band usually consists of bass, guitar, drums, and keyboards. Some larger shows hire for horn positions.

The cruise ship band backs up different performers that come in, some are name performers, some are not. As a band member, you will back up singers and performers such as comedians that perform in the main showroom or lounge.

Some ships have three or four showroom/lounges, thus opening up the floor for more jobs.

If you are a solo performer such as a singer, you can also apply for a headliner position, where you travel in, bringing your charts, perform your show, and fly out at the next port.

If you are a backing musician, you will be required to sign on for a three month contract.

This means you will be living on the ship for 90 days, and you will have very little time off.

Musicians on cruise ships work seven nights a week.

Sometimes as a musician you will be asked to work at other jobs, like helping out on deck with games and recreation activities. You need to establish up front what, if any other duties you will be asked to perform.

Living on a ship is quite an adjustment. As big as these floating hotels can be, they seem smaller and smaller with each passing week you spend on them.

The hours you play in the show will be offset by the many long hours you will spend in your cabin, usually way below deck in the dark bowels of the ship. Accommodations are cramped, and noisy. You may have to room with another band mate, and noise from the adjacent cabins can go almost non-stop.

Add to this the noise a ship makes while cruising plus noise from crew and staff, well, even earplugs won't save you. (Lower frequency noise like bass from adjacent stereo systems and forklifts running in the galley will bleed right through. If you are not a light sleeper and noise doesn't bother you, than this is a plus.)

Jerry Thomas is a guitarist from Los Angeles. He had this to say about his cruising experience:

"I did two months on a cruise ship and was more miserable than I've ever been in my life. I don't think I ever got one good night's sleep. The disposition of the people who worked on the ship was really nasty. It's a hard life and its boredom is punctuated only by the passing of idle gossip."

"The food is really not great either, because no, you don't get to eat with the passengers. All that lobster and crab and steak is for them, not for you. You will get to eat in a small 'mess' room somewhere below deck with your fellow crew members, and your choice of food will be limited. It's not all bad, trust me, but it's not the consummate dining experience the passengers are getting above deck."

But I have friends working on cruise ships that sign up year after year, and some of their interviews are included in this section.

On the other hand, Brian Lomax, a drummer in a show band on a similar line, was all raves:

"Look at it like this. You are getting paid to see the world, and you're learning your craft. Your also saving money. I use my off time during the day to get physically fit in the gym, and am writing a book. Between working out and writing, plus having lots of time for reading, I never get bored."

A Word About Sex and Crushing

Many musicians are under the mistaken notion that a cruise ship is going to be a non-stop orgy. Think again. Many cruise lines have strict rules against fraternizing with the customers (called "Coning" in the business). Being cavalier and smiling and speaking with the passengers as you are coming and going is perfectly fine, or sitting at a table with a passenger on a break is acceptable, but the hard and fast rule is that if you are seen going into a passenger's cabin, or they into yours, you will be fired and put off at the next port with a ticket home, no questions asked.

Why, You may Ask?

The answer is really about lawsuits and liability. Cruise lines are regularly sued by female passengers who claim they have been raped by cruise ship employees. Cruise lines limit this liability factor by making sure their employees are not roped into a bad situation that may end up costing the cruise line many hundreds of thousands of dollars. In a sense, the no sex policy protects everyone.

Jerry Thomas Offers:

"The cruise ship I worked on had a security force that watched us like hawks. Hallways and cabin areas were monitored by video, and if they caught any of the staff with a passenger or going into a passenger's cabin, the offending staff member was fired, and kicked off the ship at the next port."

"Also, some cruise ships tend to be populated by couples and families rather than singles, so opportunities are limited for singles to hook up. If and when single women travel together they tend to stick together and not 'slip away' with a stranger, unless the stranger is an officer."

"An officer is a member of the staff, usually wearing a really nifty pressed white naval uniform, which is a joke because they never served in any real military regiment. They really think they are something, with egos to match. If anyone gets laid, it's usually them, and security won't bother the brass."

Is there still a chance of a lowly musician finding love on the ship?

There can be, but be careful. If you take a cruise ship gig because you think you are going to get laid a lot, you are likely to be very disappointed. As one friend of mine put it, "It ain't no love boat."

If you are a loner, this can be a good gig. You are away from friends and family and your support network for months at a time, sometimes not able to see home for anymore than a day out of a month. It can get very lonely on a cruise ship.

But if you like to travel, are adventurous, are young and have no ties to home, cruising might be the ideal gig for you.

Pay

A cruise ship gig for a musician working in the house band or orchestra runs anywhere from $200–$500 per week. Keep in mind your room is rent free and your meals are free, so unless you are a big spender in port, you can save a lot of money if you hang in there.

Performers such as singers and comedians can command $1000–$2000 a night, depending on the act. Name acts can make much more, but these figures give you some idea.

PROS: Work full time, travel, save money.

CONS: Living on a ship can get old quick. Isolated from friends and family.

Types Of Gigs and What They Pay

Orchestra Musician—Back up for cabaret acts every night in addition to playing traditional Big Band type dance music. Must read.

Night Club Band—Which plays Top 40-Pop in the lounge.

Calypso Musicians—Reggae and island music consisting of steel drums, guitar, keyboards and bass. Usually a deck band that plays outside.

Strolling Musicians—Usually on higher priced cruises, they stroll through the dining room and play vocal-acoustic type music.

Piano Bar Entertainer—A singer that plays piano.

Cocktail Pianist or Intermissionist, plays piano but does not sing, usually in the atrium or dining room.

A broad range of pay for these positions would be $300–$1500 a week.

There are also Cabaret or Headliners on every ship, generally three, that ranges from Comedy, Juggling, Magic, to Singing, such as a Vocalist. The Cabaret acts usually start at $1500–$10,000 a week. These are sometimes called "Fly-Ons" These acts generally perform two nights out of the week, two shows per night.

Solo Acts need charts of their show for the orchestra to read. These are usually scored for 8 pieces: Guitar, Drums, Bass, Piano, Trumpet, Trombone, Sax and Clarinet.

If you have a new act, make sure you have your charts done before you start sending your package out: the ship that contacts you will likely need you at a moment's notice and if you have to have charts done it will take 1–2 months. Imagine the embarrassment of having to turn down a job because you don't have charts.

Cabaret positions are really the cream of the crop jobs for solo acts. They live in passenger cabins, are treated as guests, eat in the main dining room, and do not have to stay on the ship because they are only performing two nights.

Some ships require solo acts to be on the ship for the full week on one-week cruises, even though they are only performing two nights. One reason for this is that some ships don't stop at any ports mid-week. The other reason is because it costs less money to fly an act to one major port, rather than to fly them to smaller more out of the way airports, which often involve two flights or helicopter, transit.

How and Who To Contact

There are two ways to approach the cruise lines. You can approach them directly, or you can go through one of the many entertainment agencies that pitch acts to cruise lines. If you are good with business, it's always better to go direct and save the 10%–15% booking fee an agent charges.

Each cruise line has a business office based in their home port. Many of the lines are based in Miami, Florida, but they are also found worldwide.

Contact the business office of each cruise line and ask for the Entertainment Director's name, that you would like to submit a package with a demo tape.

The person answering the phone will usually give you a name and address to send your package to. It's always better to call ahead and get this info so you will be able to follow up directly with the Entertainment Director.

Keep in mind the cruise lines are swamped with an overwhelming avalanche of phone calls and packages from agents and musicians. Many of them will file your materials away until the need arises for your particular specialty.

What They Look For

Whether you go direct or through an agent, your press kit must be professional and include your:

- Bio
- Photo
- Video

Cruise lines are looking for enthusiastic, attractive people to represent the cruise line while onboard the ship. You should be healthy, reasonably fit, and have a friendly and outgoing personality.

Make sure your press kit reflects these traits.

Your video should be a short, edited 10 minute presentation showing your abilities and if possible, your interaction with your fellow musicians, or, in the case of solo acts, your interaction with the audience.

The video is the most important aspect of your package. Make sure it is professionally shot and edited, and that it shows you at your best. Always make sure it is shot in front of a live audience, showing the audience reaction to what you are doing.

Also, get your passport done in advance of applying to the ships. It can take 21 days to get a passport if you are not in a major city. If you are offered a job and you don't have a passport, you won't get the job.

Final Thoughts

Cruising is a great way to travel, meet new people, see the world and get paid for it.

It's also a good way to save money, since your room and board are paid for and there aren't a lot of places to spend money except in port.

It is also not for everyone. Speak with other musicians who are working for or have worked for the same line as you are applying. There can be a big difference between ships as their clientele can vary radically.

Find out what it's really like before you commit to a contract. 3–6 months may not sound like a long time, but it's a long time to be unhappy.

Cruise Ship Info

CRUISE SHIP INFORMATION CENTER
http://www.cruising.org/index.cfm

A COMPLETE LISTING OF CRUISE LINES
http://www.cruising.org/CruiseLines/index.cfm

Cruise Ship Booking Agencies—USA

Note: Many cruise lines prefer to be contacted directly by entertainers, and you will usually get better results going direct. However, here are a list of agencies to contact should you decide to go this route. Never pay any agency any upfront fees, they make their commission when they book you.

BRAMSON ENTERTAINMENT BUREAU
630 9th Avenue #203
New York City, NY 10036
http://www.bramson.com/index-flash.html
Phone: (212)265-3500; Fax: (212)265-6615

DON CASINO
19511 NE 19th Court
North Miami FL 33179
(305)-931-7552
http://www.doncasino.com

FIRST CLASS ENTERTAINMENT
483 Ridgewood Road
Maplewood NJ 07040-2136
(973) 763-0591
http://www.gotofirstclass.com

NEAL HOLLANDER AGENCY
9936 Majorca Place
Boca Raton, Fl 33434
http://www.nealhollanderagency.com
Voice: 561-482-1400

PROSHIP ENTERTAINMENT
Montreal PQ Canada
http://www.proship.com
Tel: (514) 485-8823

Fax: (514) 485-2675
You can also call us toll free: 1-888-477-6744
info@proship.com

SHOWMASTERS
31740 Elders Mill Road
Senoia, GA 30276

SPOTLIGHT ENTERTAINMENT
2121 N. Bayshore
Dr. #909 Miami Fl
FL 33137-5135

Helpful Websites

GETTING STARTED IN THE CRUISE LINE
INDUSTRY
http://www.jcoston.bizland.com/cruistxtfr.htm#List

CRUISE LINES INTERNATIONAL ASSOCIATION
Comprehensive listing of all cruise lines and phone
numbers
http://www.cruising.org

CRUISE LINES/ENTERTAINMENT OPERATIONS MANAGERS

Bora Bora Cruises
4347 Van Nuys Blvd
Sherman Oaks, CA 91403
www.boraborapearlcruises.com
Email: info@boraborapearlcruises.com
818-907-7981

Carnival Cruise Lines
Carnival Place, 3655 NW 87th Avenue
Miami, FL 33178-2428
www.carnival.com
Email: guestinfo@carnival.com
305-599-2600 or 1-800-438-6744
Ask For Operations Department
Rob King—Solo Acts/Cabaret
Chuck Farmer—Showbands/Musicians

Celebrity Cruises
1050 Caribbean Way
Miami, FL 33132
www.celebritycruises.com
Michael Thomas—Entertainment Head
305-539-6000

Costa Cruises
200 South Park Avenue
Hollywood, FL 33021
www.costacruises.com
Email: info@us.costa.it
954-266-5600

Crystal Cruises
Crystal Cruises
2049 Century Park East #1400
Los Angeles, CA 90067
www.crystalcruises.com
Email: mfletcher@crystalcruises.com
Sheila Hoffman—Entertainment Dept.
310-785-9300

Cunard Line
6100 Blue Lagoon Dr.
Suite 400 Miami, FL 33126
www.cunard.com
305-463-3000
Entertainment Dept: Martin Lilly
Attn: "Entertainers"
No Phone Calls Please/Send Package

Disney Cruise Line
P.O. Box 10210
Buena Vista, FL 32830
www.disneycruise.com
Email: dcl.guest.communications@disney.com
407-566-7000

First European Cruises
95 Madison Avenue
Suite 609 New York, NY 10016
www.first-european.com
Email: reser@first-european.com
212-779-7168   or
1-888-983-8767

Fred. Olsen Cruise Lines
P.O. Box 342
New York, NY 10014
www.fredolsencruises.com
Email: info@thecruisebroker.net
1-888-875-5880

Holland America Lines
300 Elliott Avenue West
Seattle, WA 98119
www.hollandamerica.com
206-281-3535

MSC Italian Cruises
250 Moonachie Road
Moonachie, NJ 07074
www.msccruisesusa.com
Email: lschnorrbusch@msc.us
201-440-4360

Norwegian Coastal Voyage Inc./Bergen Line Services
405 Park Avenue
Suite 904, New York, NY 10022
www.coastalvoyage.com
Email: info@coastalvoyage.com
212-319-1300

Norwegian Cruise Line
7665 Corporate Center Drive
Miami, FL 33126
www.ncl.com; Email: reservations@ncl.com
Attn: Michael Suman—Manager Of Music
(305) 436-4683

Oceania Cruises, Inc
8120 NW. 53rd Street
Suite 100, Miami, FL 33166
www.oceaniacruises.com
Email: customerinfo@oceaniacruises.com
305-514-2300

Orient Lines
7665 Corporate Center Drive
Miami, FL 33126
www.orientlines.com
800-327-9020

Princess
24305 Town Center Drive
Santa Clarita, CA 91355
www.princess.com
661-753-0000

Radisson Seven Seas Cruises
6000 Corporate Drive
Suite 410, Fort Lauderdale, FL 33334
www.rssc.com
Email: salesservice@radisson.com
954-776-6123

Royal Caribbean International
1050 Caribbean Way
Miami, FL 33132
www.royalcaribbean.com
Attn: Robin Cahill—Entertainment Operations Manager
http://www.royalcaribbeanproductions.com

Royal Olympia Cruises
805 3rd Avenue,
18th Floor
New York, NY 10022
www.royalolympiacruises.com
1-800-872-6400

Silversea Cruises
110 East Broward Blvd.
Fort Lauderdale, FL 33301
www.silversea.com
1-800-722-9955

Swan Hellenic
631 Commack Road
Suite 1A
Commack, NY 11725
www.swanhellenic.com
Email: swanhellenic@kainyc.com
877-219-4239

The Yachts of Seabourn
6100 Blue Lagoon Drive
Suite 400
Miami, FL 33126
www.seabourn.com
Email: fsansone@cunardmail.com
305-463-3000

Windstar Cruises
300 Elliott Ave. West
Seattle, WA 98119
www.windstarcruises.com
Email: info@windstarcruises.com
206-286-3535

Cruise Ship Entertainment Director Interviews

Robin Cahill
Royal Caribbean Cruises
Phone: (305)539-6741
Fax: (305)358-9295
1050 Caribbean Way
Miami, FL 33132

WHAT IS YOUR POSITION AT "RCCL"?

Manager, Entertainment Operations. I recruit, hire and schedule all contract entertainment for our ships and shoreside special events. I also produce the Krooze Komic program and oversee the live music program for our fleet.

WHAT JOB POSITIONS DO YOU OFFER HEADLINERS?

We have variety acts that support our Welcome, Farewell and mid week Variety shows. They are comics, jugglers, novelty acts, balancing acts, cirque type entertainment, instrumentalists, and comedy magic acts. We also book Headliners who do their own shows. We have variety and headline performers on all 19 ships.

Contracts can run anywhere from 1 week to 3 weeks to 45 weeks, depending on the individual. Some prefer to book long term, others only want a few weeks per year. I book ahead and then fill in during the year when I have fall outs or when there are itinerary changes. I will start booking 2005 this July and am usually done by September.

WHAT ARE THE PAY RANGES FOR EACH?

Variety Acts earn from $1000–$3500 per week. Head-liners earn anywhere from $3500 per week to $20,000 per week.

DO YOU REQUIRE CABARET SINGERS TO BRING THEIR OWN CHARTS?

Yes—we hope they are legible.

FOR FLY ONS, WHAT DO YOU GENERALLY LOOK FOR?

Anyone can do a fly on, however, I don't utilize a lot of fly ons as it is expensive for us. On long cruises (cruises over 7 days) to cabin issues, I do fly mid cruise acts in—I work on a sliding pay scale for those. Variety acts are typically booked from embarkation day to debarkation day—that way they can be utilized throughout the cruise as needed. Most of the more expensive. Headline acts I hire work mid cruise to mid cruise on 7 night cruises or the end of one cruise into the beginning of the next cruise on longer cruises.

WHAT TYPES OF CABARET SHOWS DO YOU LOOK FOR? BROADWAY? MUSICALS?

I prefer corporate acts as they balance better with our Broadway and Vegas style production shows. I have stand up comedy, comedy juggling, comedy magic, magic and illusion, instrumentalists, impressionists and some singers. I also book a lot of groups, such as: The Drifters, The Platters, Beatlemania, The Diamonds, The Happenings. We do not book Elvis impersonators.

WHAT IS THE BEST WAY FOR MUSICIANS AND SINGERS TO CONTACT YOU?

Email or send a package to our corporate offices, to my attention.

HOW OFTEN SHOULD MUSICIANS AND SINGERS FOLLOW UP WITH YOU ONCE THEY HAVE SENT THEIR STUFF?

I will contact them if I am interested. I don't mind email follow ups from time to time.

DEMO TAPES

VHS or CDRom work for me.

DO YOU USE AGENTS AT ALL?

I use a lot of agents—all over the world. I book over 150 acts per week.

DO YOU HIRE BIG NAME ACTS?

Yes.

WHAT ABOUT CHARTS?

Yes, they still need them, or some provide all of their own music, i.e. Peter Noone. Some bring their shows on DAT and click with the orchestra.

WHAT IS THE BIGGEST PROBLEM YOU ENCOUNTER WHEN HIRING MUSICIANS?

Rob can answer that one better than I—he hires all of our contract musicians.

ANY ADVICE FOR NEWCOMERS TO THE INDUSTRY? (YOUR PARTING SHOT)

Do your homework. You can learn about RCI on the web, through our website, or our Production Website, royalcaribbeanproductions.com. We work with many different agents and management companies. We only hire professionals who have done professional, corporate type work. If you do not have a proper package, then we recommend you invest in one. If your show is not polished and ready to go, break it in on other smaller cruise lines where the pressure not so intense.

If you are a singer and you have not developed a show, hire a writer/director to help you—the patter and segues are just as important as the songs you choose. Comics, you must have a minimum of 20 minutes of clean well produced family friendly material. Those comics that have more than 20 minutes are more valuable in this industry. Most comics support Welcome, Farwell Shows and do a 30 minutes late night. Late night does not have to be dirty.

Robert Waterfield Royal Caribbean Cruise Lines

Rob Waterfield
Specialist, Contracted Musicians
Royal Caribbean Cruises
Phone: (305)539-6741
Fax: (305)358-9295
rwaterfield@rccl.com
1050 Caribbean Way
Miami FL 33132

WHAT IS YOUR POSITION AT "Royal Caribbean"?

Contract Musician Specialist. The musicians I hire are contracted entertainers such as guitar soloists, piano bar, pub entertainer, top 40 show bands, quartets, Latin band trios and quartets. These are bands that come and they're paid once a week by check to the leader or to the agent and the whole band gets their check through one person, as opposed to musicians such as intermissionists who are on 4–6 month contracts that are paid twice a month in cash by the purser onboard.

WHAT ARE THE PAY RANGES FOR EACH?

I do the offering and negotiating of pay for the contracted musicians. Employee musicians do their pay offer/negotiations through Human Resources. I'll discuss ballpark figures with people when they call in. It's really a range, and I don't like to publish figures since every caliber of talent is worth different amounts. Suffice to say, we pay a competitive, fair wage for talent.

WHAT JOB POSITIONS DO YOU OFFER HEADLINERS?

I don't handle the headliners, they are hired through Robin Cahill. Her number is 305-539-6874.

DO YOU USE TRIBUTE ACTS?

Sometimes, depending on the act. For instance, we don't really use Elvis tributes because we cover Elvis in our review shows, which are self-contained on the ships. We have hired tribute acts such as Herb Reed's Platters.

DO YOU USE AGENTS?

I work with both agents and also directly with the musicians.

IN A VARIETY ACT WHAT DO YOU LOOK FOR? BROADWAY? MUSICALS?

We want something different from whatever we have in the on board review show. We need entertainers not just singers, people with the ability to do capture the audience. In the comedian area, we need clean comedy. In comedy, we stay away from politically incorrect humor, nothing offensive. We work with jugglers, magicians, and comics. Everybody loves Broadway, but we usually have that in the regular shows. Things go in cycles. Right now Disco and Motown are big.

WHAT IF YOU HAD A SINGER THAT COVERED ALL THE STYLES?

It's all about the "IT" factor, really, if the person can entertain the crowd, it's all about the charisma the person brings to the stage. We had a singer, Kenny James from Starsearch, he was quite dynamic.

WHAT IS THE BEST WAY FOR MUSICIANS AND SINGERS TO CONTACT YOU?

For show bands and variety acts, they should call first and then send a video, such as a quick trailer of their show or act. But then after that, on the same tape, I need to see a full show on video. This is more important for comics than for a standard musical unit. The main concern is that they don't do anything inappropriate for our guests. Avoid the MTV flashy editing; I want to have more than a few seconds.

ANY ADVICE FOR NEWCOMERS TO THE INDUSTRY? (YOUR PARTING SHOT)

So many venues have dried up over the years for live musicians, that the cruise ships offer a great opportunity today for musicians wishing to work full time. The live music business was also hurt by 9/11, and so the ships now are really a growth business. Put a decent resume together, with experience, education, references, photos, audio, DVD, as much as you can and have a good video done. If you don't have a video, send a photo, as well as a song list.

The smartest thing I've seen is for people to get a website, because then I can see right away what they have, and it can be updated quickly. Also remember the lifestyle can be difficult on a ship, you are living with employees from 52 nations. But it can be the opportunity of a lifetime.

Rob King, Carnival Cruise Lines

Carnival Cruise Lines
3655 NW 87th Avenue
Miami, FL 33178
Attn: Entertainment Dept.

WHAT IS YOUR JOB TITLE?

Musical Entertainment Manager.

HOW LONG HAVE YOU HELD IT?

Twelve years. I started out as a musician on Carnival's cruise ships, for eight years, and then I was offered a position in the main office. I hire all the musicians and bands, and **Chris Prideaux** (pronounced Pri-Dough) handles Cabaret and headliners. We also handle all the in-house shows as well.

WHAT IS THE CURRENT STATE OF THE CRUISE LINE INDUSTRY WITH REGARDS TO THE HIRING OF MUSICIANS AND SINGERS?

Good for musicians. Not as good for singers, at least on Carnival. Some lines have cut back on live music. But many lines have added ships and increased capacity, so this is the biggest growth period we've seen, so demand has increased. We have 20 ships.

WHAT JOB POSITIONS DO YOU OFFER MUSICIANS AND SINGERS?

Standard positions for house band, we have eight to 10 piece bands on our ships. It's great for young musicians learning their craft.

For singers looking to work in a in house production show it's a good market, all the cruise lines are putting a lot of money into these large lavish production shows, usually using about four to five singers in each show. We have a really wide demographic on Carnival, so we have to appeal to a wide range of musical tastes. Tribute acts don't really work on Carnival. Singers on our line have to interact with the crowd. On other lines, tributes might work.

WHAT IS THE PAY RANGE FOR MUSICIANS?

Weekly, usually around $500 per week.

WHAT POSITIONS ARE IN THE MOST DEMAND?

Piano and keyboard players who can read.

HOW MANY MUSICIAN/SINGER JOB POSITIONS DOES THE CRUISE LINE HAVE? ARE THESE POSITIONS FAIRLY HIGH TURNOVER?

Yes. Most contracts run 4–6 months, and most people move on, although we have some career people.

DO YOU REQUIRE MUSICIANS HAVE PRIOR CRUISE SHIP EXPERIENCE?

No.

DO YOU REQUIRE CABARET SINGERS TO BRING THEIR OWN CHARTS?

Yes.

WHAT INSTRUMENTATION IS REQUIRED OF THE CHARTS?

Rhythm section and 3 to 6 horns.

HOW LONG ARE THE CONTRACTS GENERALLY?

4–6 months.

WHAT IS THE BEST WAY FOR MUSICIANS AND SINGERS TO CONTACT YOU?

Send an audio tape. A video is also acceptable.

HOW OFTEN SHOULD MUSICIANS AND SINGERS FOLLOW UP WITH YOU ONCE THEY HAVE SENT THEIR STUFF?

Once a month.

DO YOU USE AGENTS AT ALL?

Not usually.

HOW MANY SHIPS?

Twenty.

ANY ADVICE FOR NEWCOMERS TO THE INDUS-TRY? (YOUR PARTING SHOT)

Be persistent, timing is everything; present the most professional package you can. Presentation is nice but the content is the most important. Make it professional. Make sure it's the best you can do, put your strongest material up front. You have about one minute to impress. Excerpts of three or four songs are good.

Chris Prideaux, Director Headline Entertainment Carnival Cruise Lines

Carnival Cruise Lines
3655 NW 87th Avenue
Miami, FL 33178
Attn: Entertainment Dept.

WHAT IS YOUR POSITION AT CARNIVAL?

I handle the headliner and cabaret entertainment, which we call fly-on entertainers.

WHAT JOB POSITIONS DO YOU OFFER HEADLINERS?

I hire acts for the showrooms, and the entertainers ideally are comedians, jugglers, ventriloquists, and illusionists. Unlike most cruise lines, our entertainers fly into the ship do their shows and get off at the next port of call, where the next entertainers get on. They are out maybe 2–3 nights at most. This way I can take my talent pool and use them on

3–4 ships per week, which usually means more money for the entertainers.

WHAT ARE THE PAY RANGES FOR EACH?

Vocalists, I don't use too many of them, but if I do hire a singer what I look for is a high energy dynamic performer, they do their own 50 minute show, performing twice, early and late seating.

We pay a daily rate, typically $200 a day. Your last day I pay $100 for travel day. Two nights pays about $500 including travel day.

DO YOU REQUIRE CABARET SINGERS TO BRING THEIR OWN CHARTS?

Yes.

FOR FLY ONS, WHAT DO YOU GENERALLY LOOK FOR?

We have 2 nights per week we call variety nights, on every ship we have production shows we already feature singers in house, so we look for comedians, jugglers, ventriloquists, illusionists, 50–55 minutes long, on variety nights I have 2 performers in, each act doing a 25 minute spot. Comedians are requested to do an adult rated late show. They need a 30-minute "clean" set and then an additional R-rated set. It's tough for comics, I expect a 10% success rate out of new comics, it's that difficult. It's a real specific art entertaining a cruise ship audience.

WHAT TYPES OF CABARET SHOWS DO YOU LOOK FOR? BROADWAY? MUSICALS?

I'm having good luck with Motown singers right now. No jazz singers or impersonators. Standards don't work for us, neither does Broadway. Big band is dead. The audience just isn't there. Whatever you do, my goal is to make 100% of the audience happy, and that's hard to do. A singer has to have a dynamic personality.

WHAT IS THE BEST WAY FOR MUSICIANS AND SINGERS TO CONTACT YOU?

By phone, call me and pitch your act. Make sure you have a demo ready to send.

HOW OFTEN SHOULD MUSICIANS AND SINGERS FOLLOW UP WITH YOU ONCE THEY HAVE SENT THEIR STUFF?

Once a month.

DEMO TAPES

I like to see a whole show on a tape; a 3-minute video doesn't show how they interact with an audience.

DO YOU USE AGENTS AT ALL?

Not usually.

116   THE MUSICIAN'S AND SINGER'S SURVIVAL GUIDE

DO YOU HIRE BIG NAME ACTS?

We've used Charro, John Davidson, Norm Crosby, but generally we don't really hire a lot of big names. It's hard to make the numbers work. On other lines, larger name acts would do well. Sometimes, on longer cruises I can use acts like these. I usually only have a budget for one name entertainer, meaning one cabin, so we can't usually accommodate more than one name person.

WHAT ABOUT CHARTS?

A must, and they have to be fully orchestrated, not lead sheets. You have one-hour rehearsal with the band prior to the show. The act must know their music and charts inside and out.

WHAT IS THE BIGGEST PROBLEM YOU ENCOUNTER WHEN HIRING MUSICIANS?

Alcoholism. You have a lot of free time on board. A lot of guys end up drunks, and it becomes a killer cycle.

ANY ADVICE FOR NEWCOMERS TO THE INDUSTRY? (YOUR PARTING SHOT)

You should be persistent but don't be a pest. There's no great mystery getting a cruise ship gig, it's just timing, really. Never ever call a booker and ask for an address and then say, "Hold a minute I have to get something to write on." Prove to me you are really serious about getting the gig. Call early in the morning. Most musicians roll out of bed and make the calls after noon, and it gets busy here afternoons. Working on a cruise ship can be productive, and a great lifestyle. All cruise lines operate differently when it comes to what they look for. Research the cruise line before you pitch your act, and make sure your act fits the venue. Too many people call me and say their act would be perfect for my line, but they are entirely misinformed, because they haven't taken the time to see if it will be a fit. Go on a three day cruise on the line you want to work for.

Micheal Suman, Norwegian Cruise Lines

Norwegian Cruise Lines—America
Attn: Micheal Suman, Manager of Music
7665 Corporate Center Drive
Miami, FL 33126 USA
(305) 436-4683
http://www.ncl.com
msuman@ncl.com

FIRST OF ALL, THANK YOU FOR CONSENTING TO THIS INTERVIEW!

My pleasure.

WHAT IS YOUR JOB TITLE?

Manager of Music.

HOW LONG HAVE YOU HELD IT?

I've been with NCL for 15 years. I've been a manager shoreside for 10.

WHAT IS THE CURRENT STATE OF THE CRUISE LINE INDUSTRY WITH REGARDS TO THE HIRING OF MUSICIANS AND SINGERS?

Very healthy. This is the only real growth area for live music. The cruise lines offer steady year round full time employment. We are also keeping the art of Cabaret alive. I don't think any other industry can say that.

WHAT JOB POSITIONS DO YOU OFFER MUSICIANS AND SINGERS?

We have Orchestra Musician, the guys that back up our cabaret acts every night in addition to playing traditional Big Band type dance music.

We have Night Club Band, which plays Top 40-Pop. We have Calypso Musicians, those are the deck bands that play outside.

We have Strolling Musicians, we use them on the higher priced cruises, where they stroll through the dining room and play vocal-acoustic type music.

Piano Bar Entertainer, which is a singer that plays piano. We have another one called Cocktail Pianist or Intermissionist, he plays piano but does not sing, usually in the atrium or dining room. A broad range of pay for these positions would be $300–$1500 a week.

We have Cabaret or Headliners on every ship, generally three, that ranges from Comedy, Juggling, Magic, to Singing, such as a Vocalist. The Cabaret acts usually start at $1500–$10,000 a week. These are sometimes called "Fly-Ons" on other lines, but we require the act stay on the ship for the full week, even though they will perform two nights. So they really aren't considered "fly-ons" in the traditional sense of the word.

WHAT POSITIONS ARE IN THE MOST DEMAND?

It varies, but night club and band positions, usually.

HOW MANY MUSICIAN/SINGER JOB POSITIONS DOES THE CRUISE LINE HAVE?

Two hundred twenty five at the moment.

ARE THESE POSITIONS FAIRLY HIGH TURNOVER?

The turnover rate is about three times per year, I lose maybe 25% per year, but I fill them fast.

DO YOU REQUIRE MUSICIANS HAVE PRIOR CRUISE SHIP EXPERIENCE?

No.

DO YOU REQUIRE CABARET SINGERS TO BRING THEIR OWN CHARTS?

Yes.

WHAT INSTRUMENTATION IS REQUIRED OF THE CHARTS?

Seven pieces, four rhythm (guitar, bass, drums, keys) and three horns (sax, trumpet, trombone).

HOW LONG ARE THE CONTRACTS GENERALLY?

One week to six months

ARE PAY RAISES POSSIBLE?

Yes.

ARE POSITIONS AVAILABLE FOR SINGERS WITH THEIR OWN SHOWS?

Yes, these are the Cabaret and Headliner positions.

WHAT TYPES OF CABARET SHOWS DO YOU LOOK FOR? BROADWAY? MUSICALS?

Starsearch-winner type material. For Europe, it's usually Broadway, for our Carribbean ships it's more pop-oriented.

HOW LONG ARE THE SETS FOR A CABARET SINGER?

Two shows, a 55 minute full show, and a 20 minute show.

WHAT IS THE BEST WAY FOR MUSICIANS AND SINGERS TO CONTACT YOU?

Send a promo packet with an edited video tape, no longer than 10–15 minutes.

HOW OFTEN SHOULD MUSICIANS AND SINGERS FOLLOW UP WITH YOU ONCE THEY HAVE SENT THEIR STUFF?

I personally review everything within two weeks of receiving it. The information goes into a database, and when I need that particular position or act filled, I will pursue the quality acts. Follow up is not needed, if it's a great act, I will be in touch. If the act is not up to our standards, we will not contact you.

DO YOU USE AGENTS AT ALL?

Yes, but it is not necessary. They can simply send the promo to our home office. A video is essential.

DO YOU HIRE BIG NAME ACTS?

Yes.

WHAT IS THE BIGGEST PROBLEM YOU ENCOUNTER WHEN HIRING MUSICIANS?

With orchestra positions they tend to stop learning songs past 1950. The colleges don't teach contemporary music.

The biggest problem with Night Club Bands is there aren't many great ones. There are thousands of marginal ones, though.

ANY ADVICE FOR NEWCOMERS TO THE INDUSTRY? (YOUR PARTING SHOT)

Ship life can be easy, you roll out of bed, everything is done for you. But it can also be hard being away from family and loved ones.

One of the problems I see is some guys never leave. They stay on the ship for 10–20 years and live a very insulated life. But it's a life you can get used to. The first week is the toughest, they see the size of their cabin and they panic, but after a week or so they make friends and want to stay eight months. It's not the kind of job that's suited for people who are set in their ways and not used to institutionalized life. It's hard for people who have lived on their own and are not used to roomates, rules and regulations.

Go ahead and assume you are of quality enough to get the job, don't be afraid, it's not a bad lifestyle, and you will bank a lot of money because you have no expenses. Your food and board are all taken care of. You'll see the world and learn a lot.

And if you're good, we need you.

Cruise Ship Booking Resources

Note: Many cruise lines prefer to be contacted directly by entertainers, and you will usually get better results going direct. However, here are a list of agencies to contact should you decide to go this route. Never pay any agency any upfront fees, they make their commission when they book you.

Bramson Entertainment Bureau
630 9th Avenue #203
New York City, NY 10036
http://www.bramson.com/index-flash.html
Phone: (212) 265-3500
Fax: (212) 265-6615

Don Casino
19511 NE 19th Court North
Miami, FL 33179
(305)-931-7552
http://www.doncasino.com

First Class Entertainment
483 Ridgewood Road
Maplewood, NJ 07040-2136
(973) 763-0591
http://www.gotofirstclass.com

Neal Hollander Agency
9936 Majorca Place
Boca Raton, Fl 33434
http://www.nealhollanderagency.com
Voice: 561-482-1400

Proship Entertainment
Montreal PQ Canada
http://www.proship.com
Tel: (514) 485-8823
Fax: (514) 485-2675
You can also call us toll free: 1-888-477-6744
info@proship.com

Showmasters
31740 Elders Mill Road Senoia
GA 30276

Spotlight Entertainment
2121 N. Bayshore, Dr. #909
Miami Fl, FL 33137-5135

Helpful Websites

Getting Started in the Cruise Line Industry
http://www.jcoston.bizland.com/cruistxtfr.htm#List

Cruise Lines International Association
Comprehensive listing of all cruise lines and phone numbers
http://www.cruising.org

CHAPTER 11

Interviews

Liberty Music—A Philadelphia Story: From Musician To Booking Agent

Concert Promoters—All In Black Productions

Making The Show Go: A Concert Promotion Primer—Conrad Mueller

Liberty Music—A Philadelphia Story: From Musician To Booking Agent

John McCullough is a pianist who grew up in Philadelphia, working in local groups as diverse as The Paul Christopher Band, Cook E. Jarr and the Crumbs, and a multitude of lounge and show acts.

In 1999, he formed his own small booking agency, which he ran from his apartment in the Philadelphia area, where he continues to book solo acts and ensembles in public venues such as luxury hotels and restaurants, and also on corporate and private events.

This is his story.

MARK: Hello, John. How did you get started in this business?

JOHN: I was playing in bands as a kid, really, I worked in several bands by the time I was eighteen. I was on the road with several different acts between 1978 and 1984. The problem with bands is they always fall apart at some point. So I developed my soloing skills so I could go out and play singles.

MARK: What made you decide to start booking other musicians?

JOHN: It came out of necessity, because I was already booked on dates, the places would call and I'd have to find other musicians to fill the dates.

MARK: What kind of acts do you book?

JOHN: A lot of solo piano, small jazz ensembles, harpist's classical guitar, occasionally dance bands. Basically any type of live music.

MARK: Was it an instant success?

JOHN: Not by a long shot. I struggled with it for five years before it really generated any kind of decent money. But I was always able to get gigs for myself. I just kept building my mailing list and making lots of phone calls. I did a lot of marketing and mailing, like sending out personalized calendars to my client list, boxes of Altoids, and ad specialty type of stuff. Another thing I did was getting a list of hotels, restaurants, country clubs caterers and corporations I called them, getting the name of the director of catering event planner or director of marketing, and mailed them. This is an endless job. There are thousands of these venues in the greater Philadelphia area. It also takes a long time for the gigs to come in because most of the places have never heard of you before. But eventually you establish a relationship and they give you a shot.

MARK: How is business now?

JOHN: Very good. I am working steady and book quite a few musicians each week. I don't have any employees, I run the business myself, and so I have to do everything. The next phase will be to hire someone to work in the office with me to handle the phones.

MARK: What were your goals ten years ago as compared to now?

JOHN: Making it really big in this business is not a realistic goal. I always just wanted to be the best musician and composer I could be, and to work. The music business has changed a lot, it's gotten tougher for live gigs and the economy has not been great for gigs since the late eighties. But by realizing that I have a good product, and being a good salesman my business has constantly grown. My hope now is to continue along these lines.

MARK: What kind of advice do you give new musicians?

JOHN: Try to develop something you can do as a solo act, so you aren't dependant on other musicians for your livelihood. As a keyboard or guitar player or singer, you have a lot of options in developing a solo act. If you are a singer, you can use backing tracks, lighting and even multi-media to build an exciting show around yourself. This is also true for guitarists and keyboard players. Technology has made so much possible at a lower cost than ever. Handle your own business. Agents can get you work if you are inside their inner circle, but don't bet on it. Try to go out and get your own work or develop your own gigs. Record a CD, if possible, and sell it on your gigs or give it away to your customers. I did this with a Christmas CD I recorded a year ago and it's selling great. Use the Internet; it's a great tool.

MARK: Any parting shot?

JOHN: Yeah. Keep plugging, it can take years but you can build a success story for yourself if you work the right angles. Hang in there. That's the main thing.

Derek Sivers—CD Baby

```
If you mount a toothbrush on the wall,
it's art.
```

It's art because you're making people pay attention to it and think about it.

BELOW ARE A BUNCH OF TIPS ABOUT HOW TO CALL MORE ATTENTION TO YOUR MUSIC.

They're really meant as individual "thought for the day" things. Eating them all at once could make you sick. So instead - go through this one long email slowly. Get inspired, and try some crazy idea. Just one. It'll work, and excite you. Then next week you'll try another, and another. And everyone will ask you why you're so lucky.

IMPORTANT: Nothing here is telling you to be something you're not. The goal is to just turn up the volume on who you really are so the world can hear it. Never forget you're an artist. And part of an artist's job is to call attention to what they're creating. A toothbrush in the sink isn't art. A toothbrush mounted on a wall, with a spotlight on it, and a room full of people paying attention to it, is art.

Read on ...

PLEASE FORWARD THIS EMAIL TO EVERY MUSICIAN YOU THINK DESERVES MORE ATTENTION

WHO'S WRITING THIS? Me. Derek Sivers. Musician. 32 years old. Founder of CD Baby. I've been a full-time musician for about 10 years. (Last time I had a day job was 1992.) Toured the world as a guitarist sideman with some famous folks, (played to sold-out 15,000 seat stadiums.) Toured the country in a circus, too. Ran a recording studio. Worked inside the industry at Warner/Chappell Music for 3 years. Had some really great teachers that taught me a lot about the music business. Cracked the college market and got hired by 400 colleges in 3 years. Sold a few thousand of my own CD.

And that's why I started CD Baby as a hobby: to sell my own CD and a dozen friends who needed distribution. But it accidentally took off (oops!) and now I'm in this interesting position of being "the guy behind the counter at CD Baby."

Between my past and present, I've learned a LOT about how to call attention to your music. Now I get to see what OTHER people are doing. What sells. What works. Every time someone is selling a LOT of CDs on CD Baby, I check out their website, their emails, their marketing plan. I call them up and ask, "What are you doing? How'd you do that?"

So ... HERE ARE MY COLLECTED OBSERVATIONS AND THOUGHTS ABOUT WHAT CALLS ATTENTION TO YOUR MUSIC. USE THEM!

(You might have already seen this on *http://www.MarketingYourMusic.com* - but here it is in an oh-so-convenient email. Forward it to anyone you want.)

Derek Sivers, CD Baby *http://www.cdbaby. net/derek*

P.S. A band called O.A.R. just sold 1,500 CDs in 5 days through CD Baby! That's a $15,000 check for one week. (They're 4 students. Not on TV or radio. People just LOVE their music, and tell their friends. It's all word-of-mouth.) I asked their manager how they did it and he said, "I read your tips. Checked out the books you recommended. Followed your advice. That's all."

Marketing Your Music by Derek Sivers *http://www. cdbaby.net/Derek*

######### BIG STRATEGIES ######### Derek Sivers - *http://www.cdbaby.net/derek*

CALL THE DESTINATION, AND ASK FOR DIRECTIONS.

Work backwards.

Define your goal (your final destination) - then contact someone who's there, and ask how to get there.

Know a magazine you think you should be in? Call their main number, ask for the editorial department, and ask someone in editorial if they could recommend their three favorite publicists. Write down the publicists' names, and thank the nice editorial person for their time. (Don't waste their time asking for the publicists' contact info. You can find that on the web.) Then call each publicist, and try to get their attention.

Know a radio station you should be on? Call them and ask for the music director. Ask if they could recommend a few good radio promoters. Call the radio promoters they recommend, and try to get their attention.

Know a venue you should be playing? Bring a nice box of fancy German cookies to the club booker, and ask for just 5 minutes of their advice. Ask them what criteria must be met in order for them to take a chance on an act. Ask what booking agents they recommend, or if they recommend using one at all. Again, keep your meeting as short as possible. Get the crucial info, then leave them alone. (Until you're back, headlining their club one day!)

I know an artist manager of a small unsigned act, who over the course of a year, met with the managers of U2, REM, and other top acts. She asked them for their advice, coming from the top, and got great suggestions that she's used with big results.

In other words: Call the destination, and ask for directions.

You'll get there much faster than just blindly walking out your front door, hoping you arrive someday.

PUT YOUR FANS TO WORK.

You know those loyal few people who are in the front row every time you perform? You know those people that sat down to write you an Email to say how much they love your music? You know that guy that said, "Hey if you ever need anything - just ask!"

Put them to work!

Often, people who reach out like that are looking for a connection in this world. Looking for a higher cause. They want to feel they have some other purpose than their stupid accounting job.

You may be the best thing in their life.

You can break someone out of their drab life as an assistant sales rep for a man-ufacturing company. You might be the coolest thing that ever happened to a teenager going through an unpopular phase. You can give them a mission!

If they're a fan of your music, invite them over for pizza to spend a night doing a mail-ing to colleges. Go hit the town together, putting concert flyers on telephone poles. Have them drive a van full of friends to your gig an hour away. Have the guts to ask that "email fan" if she'd be into going through the Indie Contact Bible and sending your presskit to 20 magazines a week.

Soon you can send them out on their own, to spread the gospel message of your amaz-ing music, one promo project at a time. Eventually, as you grow, these people can be the head of "street teams" of 20 peo-ple in a city that go promote you like mad each time you have a concert or a new CD.

Those of us busy busy people may think, "How could Anyone do this slave work?" But there are plenty of people out there with time on their hands that want to spend it on something besides TV.

Don't forget that to most people, the music business is pure magic. It's Hollywood. It's glitter and fame and fantastically romantic. Working with you might be the closest they get to that magical world of music. Give someone the chance to be on the inside circle. Put 'em to work.

PHOTOS OF YOUR AUDIENCE ON YOUR WEBSITE.

Secret trick to get people in the audience to sign your mailing list AND be part of your inside club.

1. At every show you do, from now on, bring a camera and a notebook.
2. About halfway through your show, when everyone is having fun, take pictures of the audience, from the stage. Tell them to smile, make a face, hold up their beer, whatever.
3. Afterwards, pass around the notebook and say, "Please write down your email address in this notebook, and in a few days, I'll email you, telling you where you can see YOUR goofy picture on my website."

4. At the end of the night, before bed, write up a journal/diary/memoir of that show. Scan and upload all their pictures onto a page of your website. Dedicate a page of your site about that show, with the diary, photos, and a little link on that page that says, "If you were at this show, please introduce yourself!" - so people can contact you.

5. Email everyone that was there that night. Of course Everyone will go look at your site. How could they not? People are infinitely more interested in themselves than they are in you.

6. Stay in touch with them all!

(p.s. The other hidden idea in this is to make every show a Real Event. A Big Deal. Something worth documenting. This will get you out of the habit of thinking of it as "just another gig." Because for many of your fans, it's not. It's the most fun they've had all month.)

Here's an example. One of my old outdated tour diaries: *http://www.hitme.net/tourdiary/*

(After starting CD Baby in 1998 I stopped touring. But since I had been on the road for 10 years straight, I'm not complaining.)

GO WHERE THE FILTERS ARE.

Have you been filtered? If not, you should start now. (Huh?)

With the internet, there are more "media outlets" than anyone can digest. A site like MP3.COM has 250,000 artists on there. Many of them are crap. People in the music biz get piles of CDs in the mail everyday from amateurs. Many of them are crap.

But you're not crap, are you? No! So prove it! Don't sit in the bin with the rest.

You need to go through filters. Places that reject many, only letting the best of the best pass through.

As long as you're good (really good) - what you want are MORE filters! More obstacles ... More hurdles ...

Because these things weed out the "bad" music. Or the music that isn't ready. Or the people that weren't dedicated.

I worked at Warner Brothers for 3 years. I learned why they never accept unso-licited demos: It helps weed out the peo-ple that didn't do enough research to know they have to go meet managers or lawyers or David Geffen's chauffeur FIRST in order to get to the "big boys." (Deal with the 'gatekeepers' to get to the mansion.)

If you REALLY REALLY BELIEVE in your music, have the confidence to put yourself into those places where MOST people get rejected. (Radio, magazines, big venues, agents, managers, record labels, promoters ...)

Because each gate you get through puts you in finer company. ("The best of the best.")

And you'll find many more opportunities open to you once you've earned your way through a few gates.

EXTREME RESULTS = EXTREME ACTIONS.

You don't get extreme talent, fame, or success without extreme actions.

Be less leisurely.

Throw yourself into this entirely.

Find what you love and let it kill you.

IF THIS IS DRAINING YOUR ENERGY, PLEASE STOP!

"Whatever scares you, go do it." ←one of my favorite slogans.

If something scares you in an excited way (something that *gives* you energy) - that's a good sign.

BUT IF SOMETHING IS MAKING YOU MISERABLE AND DRAINING YOUR ENERGY, PLEASE STOP.

Life is telling you that is not the path for you.

QUICK EXAMPLE: Biggest mistake I ever made in my life:

My band was doing well. A well-meaning lawyer that I trusted told me that I should start a record label. "Find and sign 3 other artists. Do for them what you did for your band. Then sell the whole label for a million bucks!!"

I walked out of his office with slumped shoulders, miserable, saying, "yeah ... I guess he's right ..."

With a long face, I plopped in a chair back home and thought, "Oh man ... do I really have to do this?" But because I trusted him, I spent 2 years of my life trying!

It wasn't what came natural to me, and so of course it was a failure, AND since I had spent so much time on it, the thing that I WAS good at (making music) was being ignored!!

I wish I would have paid attention to my lack of enthusiasm and stuck with the things that excited me.

Please don't make the same mistake.

If anything I'm talking about here makes you tired instead of wired, just don't do it! Stick with what excites you. That's where you'll find your success.

HAVE SOMEONE WORK THE INSIDE OF THE INDUSTRY

I prefer to ignore the music industry. Maybe that's why you don't see me on the cover of Rolling Stone.

One of my only regrets about my own band was that we toured and got great reviews, toured and got lots of airplay, toured and booked some great-paying gigs. BUT ... nobody was working the inside of the music business.

Nobody was connecting with the "gatekeepers" to bring us to the next level. We just kept doing the same gigs.

Maybe you're happy on the outside of the biz. (I know I am.)

But if you want to tour with major-label artists, be on the cover of national magazines, be in good rotation on the biggest radio stations in town, or get onto MTV, you're going to have someone working the inside of the biz.

Someone who loves it. Someone who is loved by it. Someone persuasive who gets things done 10 times faster than you ever could. Someone who's excited enough about it, that they would never be discouraged.

Like your love of making music. You wouldn't just "stop" making music because you didn't get a record deal would you? Then you need to find someone who's equally passionate about the business side of music, and particularly the business side of YOUR music.

It IS possible. There are lots of people in this world.

BE A NOVICE MARKETER, NOT AN EXPERT.

Get to the point of being a novice marketer/promoter/agent. Then hand it to an expert.

Moby, the famous techno artist, says the main reason for his success was that he found experts to do what they're best at, instead of trying to do it himself.

Paraphrased: "Instead of trying to be a booking agent, publicist, label, and manager, I put my initial energy into finding and impressing the best agent, publicist, label, and manager. And I just kept making lots of the best music I could."

If you sense you are becoming an expert, figure out what your real passions in life are and act accordingly.

Maybe you're a better publicist than bassist. Maybe you're a better bassist than publicist.

Maybe it's time to admit your weakness as a booking agent, and hand it off to someone else. Maybe it's time to admit your genius as a booking agent, and commit to it full-time.

THINK OF EVERYTHING FROM THEIR POINT OF VIEW.
Derek Sivers - *http://www.cdbaby.net/derek*

CONSTANTLY ASK, "WHAT DO THEY REALLY WANT?"

Want to know the basic rule or marketing and promoting your music?

Constantly ask, "What do they really want?" (With "they" being anyone you are trying to reach.)

Think hard, and don't take this one lightly.

Thinking of everything from the other person's point of view is a seeeerious Jedi mind trick. If done right, it will elevate you into the clouds along with a few select immortal beings.

Every time you lift up the phone. Every time you write an Email. Every time you send out a presskit.

Think why people in the music industry are REALLY working this job. Try to imagine them as just a well-meaning human being who is probably overworked, looking for a little happiness in the world, and likes music (or the music world itself) enough to do what they do, even though they could be doing something else.

Think what their Email "IN" box must look like, and how it would be unwise for you to send them an email with the subject of "hey" followed by a 7-page Email detailing your wishes for success.

Think what people are REALLY looking for when they go out to a club to hear music. For some people, it's just a way to be seem to increase their popularity. For some, they're searching for some music that does something completely original and mind-blowing. Some are looking for total visual entertainment.

Nobody owes you their attention. Not your audience. Not a person you happened to call or Email. Not even the music industry.

Let go of your ego entirely. Think of everything from their point of view. Be their dream come true. Do what they really want.

(This even goes down to the smallest levels: what kind of phone message you leave, what kind of cover letter you write in a package, what kind of subject header you put in your email.)

And maybe, just maybe, they'll be or do exactly what you want.

REACH THEM LIKE YOU WOULD WANT TO BE REACHED.

Reach people like you would want to be reached.

Would you rather have someone call you up in a dry business monotone, and start speaking a script like a telemarketer?

Or would you rather have someone be a cool person, a real person?

When you contact people, no matter how it's done (phone, email, mail, face-to-face) - show a little spunk. Stand apart from the crowd.

If it sounds like they have a moment and aren't in a major rush, entertain them a bit. Ask about their day and expect a real answer. Talk about something non-business for a minute or two.

Or - if they sound hectic, skip the "how are you", skip the long introduction, ask your damn question and move out of the way.

This means you must know your exact question before you contact them, just in case that ultra-quick situation is needed.

Reach them like you would want to be reached. Imagine what kind of phone call or Email YOU would like to get.

If you're contacting fans, imagine what kind of flyer they would like to get in their mailbox. Something dull and "just the facts" - or something a little twisted, creative, funny, entertaining and unique? Something corporate, or something artistic?

This is a creative decision on your part. Every contact with the people around your

music (fans and industry) is an extension
of your art. If you make depressing,
morose, acoustic music, maybe you should
send your fans a dark brown-and-black little understated flyer that's depressing
just to look at. Set the tone. Pull in
those people who love that kind of thing.
Proudly alienate those that don't.

If you're an in-your-face, tattooed, coun-
try-metal-speedpunk band, have the guts to
call a potential booking agent and scream,
"Listen you fucking motherfucker! I'm going
to explode! Ah! Aaaaaaah!!!" If they like
that introduction, you've found a good match.

Be different. (Even if it's just in your
remarkable efficiency.)

Everyone wants a little change in their day.

THEY KNOW NOTHING ABOUT YOU. DON'T ASSUME
ANYTHING.

People will always and forever ask you,
"What kind of music do you do?"

Musicians often say, "All styles, really."

If the stranger you said that to happens to
be a fan of African music, watch out! You
better combine the polyrhythmic drumming of
West Africa with the rich vocal harmonies

of South Africa, with the microtonal reeds of Northeast Africa. And if they have any awareness of the rest of the world, then your CD better combine rage-rap, country line dancing, Chinese opera, ambient techno trance, Hungarian folk songs, and the free jazz of Ornette Coleman. (Hey - you said "all styles" didn't you?)

This example is extreme, but constantly remember: people know nothing about you, or your background, or where you're coming from. If you say you sound "totally unique" - then you better not have any chords, drums, guitars, words, or any sounds that have ever been made in the history of music.

When you speak to the world, you are speaking to strangers from all kinds of backgrounds and tastes.

Open your mind. Realize you don't sound like all styles, and you're not totally 100% unique.

Do them a favor. Don't assume anything. Say what it is you sound like. Narrow it down a bit.

If you do this in a creative way ("We sound like the Incredible Hulk having sex.") - you can intrigue people and make them want your CD, or want to come to your next show. Whereas if you had said, "Everything" - then you didn't make a fan.

WHAT HAS WORKED ON YOU?

Any time you're trying to influence people to do something, think what has worked on YOU in the past.

Are you trying to get people to buy your CD? Write down the last 20 CDs you bought, then for each one, write down what made you buy it.

Did you ever buy a CD because of a matchbook, postcard, or 30-second web sound clip? What DID work? (Reviews, word-of-mouth, live show?)

Write down your top 10 favorite artists of all time, and a list of what made you discover each one and become a fan.

Here's where it gets heavy: Ask your friends to answer these same questions.

You'll end up with a "how-to" list, giving you 100 ideas for how to make people a lifelong fan of your music.

P.S. This goes beyond music. Which TV ads made you buy something? What anonymous

Emails made you click a link and check out a website? Which flyers or radio ads made you go and see a live show by someone you had never heard?

HAVE THE CONFIDENCE TO TARGET.
Derek Sivers - *http://www.cdbaby.net/derek*

BAD TARGETING EXAMPLE: PROGRESSIVE ROCKER TARGETING TEENYBOPPER.

On CD Baby, there is a great musician who made an amazing heavy-progressive-metal record.

When we had a "search keywords" section, asking for three artists he sounds like, he wrote, "Britney spears, Ricky martin, Jennifer Lopez, backstreet boys, mp3, sex, free."

What the hell was he thinking? He just wanted to turn up in people's search engines, at any cost.

But for what? And who?

Did he really want a Britney Spears fan to get "tricked" into finding his dark-progressive-metal record? Would that 13-year-old girl actually spend the 25 minutes to download his 10 minute epic, "Confusing

Mysteries of Hell"? If she did, would she buy his CD?

I suggested he instead have the confidence to target the REAL fans of his music.

He put three semi-obscure progressive artists into the search engine, and guess what?

He's selling more CDs than ever! He found his true fans.

IF YOU DON'T SAY WHAT YOU SOUND LIKE, YOU WON'T MAKE ANY FANS.

A person asks you, "What kind of music do you do?" Musicians say, "All styles. Everything."

That person then asks, "So who do you sound like?" Musicians say, "Nobody. We're totally unique. Like nothing you've ever heard before."

What does that person do? Nothing. They might make a vague promise to check you out sometime. Then they walk on, and for-get about you! Why??? You didn't arouse their curiosity! You violated a HUGE rule of self-promotion! Bad bad bad!

What if you had said, "It's 70's porno-funk music being played by men from Mars." Or ... "This CD is a delicate little kiss on your earlobe from a pink-winged pixie." Or ... "We sound like a cross between AC/DC and Tom Jones." Or ... "It's deep-dancing reggae that magically places palm trees and sand wherever it is played, and grooves so deep it makes all non-dancers get drunk on imaginary island air, and dance in the sand."

Any one of these, and you've got their interest.

Get yourself a magic key phrase that describes what you sound like. Try out a few different ones, until you see which one always gets the best reaction from strangers. Use it. Have it ready at a moment's notice.

It doesn't have to narrow what you do at all. Any of those three examples I use above could sound like anything.

And that's just the point - if you have a magic phrase that describes your music in curious but vague terms, you can make total strangers start wondering about you.

But whatever you do, stay away from the words "everything", "nothing", "all styles", and "totally unique".

Say something!

PROUDLY EXCLUDE SOME PEOPLE.

Proudly say what you're NOT: "If you like Celine Dion, you'll hate us."

... and people who hate Celine Dion will love you. (Or at least give you a chance.)

You can't please everyone in this world. So go ahead and recklessly leave out people.

Almost like you're the doorman at an exclusive club that plays only your music. Maybe you wouldn't let in anyone wearing a suit. Maybe you wouldn't let in anyone without a suit!

But know who you are, and have the confidence that somewhere out there, there's a little niche of people that would like your kind of music. They may only be 1% of the population. But 1% of the world is 20 million people!

Loudly leave out 99% of the world. When someone in your target 1% hears you excluding the part of the population they already feel alienated from, they'll be drawn to you.

Write down a list of artists who you don't like, and whose fans probably wouldn't like you. Use that.

THE MOST EXPENSIVE VODKA.

There is a vodka company that advertises itself as The Most Expensive Vodka You Can Buy.

I'll bet they're very successful with it. It's almost a dare. (And it proudly excludes people!)

Other companies are all trying to find ways to be the cheapest, and someone had the guts to decide that they were going to do exactly the opposite of everyone else.

There are some people who read the Billboard charts, and try to imitate the current trends and styles.

I suggest, even as an experiment, strongly declaring that you are something totally UN-trendy - the opposite from what everyone else wants or is trying to be.

154 THE MUSICIAN'S AND SINGER'S SURVIVAL GUIDE

Perhaps you could advertise your live show as, "The most boring concert you'll ever see."

Perhaps you want to call your music, "The most un-catchy, difficult to remember, un-danceable music you've ever heard."

Or tell the music industry, "This music has no hit potential whatsoever."

I'll bet you get their attention.

It's almost a dare.

IF YOU TARGET SHARP ENOUGH, YOU WILL OWN YOUR NICHE.

Let's say you've decided that your style of music should be proudly called "power-pop".

If you say, "We're powerpop!" in the very first sentence or paragraph all of your marketing. If your Email address is "powerpop@yahoo.com", if your album title is "Powerpop Drip and Drop", if the license plate on your band van is "POWRPOP".

Well then ... when someone comes into my record store and says they like powerpop, guess who I'm going to tell them to buy?

Have the confidence to find your niche, define who you are, then declare it again and again and again and again.

If you do it persistently enough, you will OWN that niche. People will not be able to imagine that niche without you.

(You can try to make your own, if you're brave. You might be "the best techno-opera artist in the world".)

GRAB PEOPLE'S ATTENTION, SENSES AND EMOTIONS
Derek Sivers - *http://www.cdbaby.net/derek*

TOUCH AS MANY OF THEIR SENSES AS YOU CAN.

The more senses you touch in someone, the more they'll remember you.

BEST: a live show, with you sweating right on top of someone, the PA system pounding their chest, the smell of the smoky club, the flashing lights and live-in-person performance.

WORST: an email, a single web page, a review in a magazine with no photo.

(Let's say that "emotions" are one of the senses.)

Whenever possible, try to reach as many senses as possible. Have an amazing photo of yourself or your band, and convince every reviewer to put that photo next to the review of your album.

Send videos with your presskit. Play live shows often. Understand the power of radio to make people hear your music instead of just hearing about it.

Get onto any TV shows you can. Scent your album with patchouli oil. Make your songs and productions truly emotional instead of merely catchy.

(Touching their emotions is like touching their body. If you do it, you'll be remembered.)

NEVER USE CORPORATE-SPEAK.

Don't try to sound pro or use industry catch phrases.

Would you do that to a friend?

Your fans are your friends. Speak to them like real people.

Write every letter or email as if it were to a good friend. From you to your best friend Beth.

Even if it's going out to 10,000 people.

LEAVE 'EM WANTING MORE.

What's more appealing?

Someone holding a carrot in front of your face, then pull it back towards them slowly?

Or someone shoving 50 carrots in your mouth?

Brian Eno (my favorite theorist) says the best thing you can do is to bring people to the point where they start searching.

Not so plain or obvious that there's nothing left to the imagination. Not so cryptic that they give up.

Give people just enough to pull them in, but make them want more. Make them go searching for clues, or details, or explanations, or "more of what you just gave me."

ALL THE WORLD'S A STAGE. WHAT CHARACTER ARE YOU?
Derek Sivers - *http://www.cdbaby.net/derek*

IMAGINE A PLAY WITH 1000 ACTORS ON STAGE.

Imagine you're in the audience of a play. Big theater. Opera house.

Imagine there are one thousand actors on stage.

Which ones would stand out? Which ones would you remember?

It's not always going to be the loudest or most hyperactive.

Maybe you'd be drawn into the misty-blue woman with the long black hair in the deep blue cape with half her face hidden, standing silently at the edge of the stage.

Now you, as a musician, are one of the actors on that overcrowded stage.

Would you stand out? Would people remember you? Are you being strong enough version of YOU, so that people who DO want who YOU are can find you in the crowd?

(P.S. The most memorable actor on stage might be the one that gets off the stage, walks up to your seat, and gives you a kiss.)

BE AN EXTREME VERSION OF YOURSELF.

Define yourself. Show your weirdness. Bring out all your quirks.

Your public persona, the image you show to the world, should be an extreme version of yourself.

EVEN CONSERVATIVE LEGENDS WERE EXTREME.

Think of the legendary performers in that conservative style. (The ones even your grandmother could like.)

Frank Sinatra. Charlie Chaplin. Liberace. Liza Minelli. Barbara Streisand.

Even the most conservative "legendary" performers were rather extreme characters.

Don't be afraid to be as extreme as you can imagine. Being in the spotlight is the excuse. You can get away with anything, all in the name of entertainment.

THINK TEST MARKETING - PROOF OF SUCCESS.
Derek Sivers - *http://www.cdbaby.net/Derek*

TEST. IMPROVE. PERFECT. ANNOUNCE.

In this indie music world, the best thing you can do is think in terms of "Test Marketing."

This is what food companies do before they release a new product. They release it just in Denver (for example), and see what people think of it there. They get feedback. They try a different name. They try an improved flavor, based on complaints or compliments. They try a different ad campaign. They see what works. Constantly improving.

When it's a huge success in Denver, they know they're on to something good. They can now release it in Portland, Dallas, and Pittsburgh. Do the same thing.

When everyone seems to like it, they get the financial backing to "roll it out" and confidently spend a ton of money to distribute it around the whole country, or the whole world. The people investing money into it are confident, because it was a huge success in all the test markets.

Think of what you're doing with your music as test marketing.

When you're a huge success on a lower level, or in a small area, THEN you can go to the big companies and ask for financial or resource help to "roll it out" to the country or world.

Then they'll feel confident that their big money is being well invested.

A GOOD BIZ PLAN WINS NO MATTER WHAT HAP-
PENS.

In doing this test marketing you should
make a plan that will make you a success
even if nobody comes along with their
magic wand.

Start now. Don't wait for a "deal".

Don't just record a "demo" that is meant
only for record companies.

You have all the resources you need to
make a finished CD that thousands of people would want to buy. If you need more
money, get it from anyone except a record
company.

And if, as you're following your great
business plan, selling hundreds, then
thousands of CDs, selling out small, then
larger venues, getting on the cover of
magazines ... you'll be doing so well that
you won't need a record deal.

And if a record deal IS offered to you,
you'll be in the fine position of taking
it or leaving it. There's nothing more
attractive to an investor than someone who
doesn't need their money. Someone who's
going to be successful whether they're
involved or not.

Make the kind of business plan that will get you to a good sustainable level of success, even without a big record deal. That way you'll win no matter what happens.

######### THE POWER OF PEOPLE. #########
Derek Sivers - *http://www.cdbaby.net/derek*

GET USED TO THE IDEA OF DATABASE AND QUANTITY.

If you want any level of success beyond the admiration of friends and family, you have to get used to the idea of dealing with great numbers of people.

One good review means almost nothing. Getting airplay on one radio station is not enough.

You need to stay in close touch with hundreds, and soon, thousands of people. Whether fans, music biz, or the endless characters you're going to encounter around the world on your way to the top, you're going to need to keep track of them all.

You're going to need a database. A "contact manager". A fancy term for "a fancy address book". An amazing tool with endless memory to help our artistic, creative, musical brains which are often lost in space and notoriously flaky.

It takes a discipline and orderliness you
may not be used to, but comes in SO handy
when you need to contact that graphic
designer who introduced himself to you
once after a gig in St. Louis a year and
a half ago. Or to be able, in 5 seconds,
to find the 28 drummers you know in north-
ern Oregon.

Get used to this concept, and we'll go
into detail on the next page.

STAY IN CLOSE TOUCH WITH HUNDREDS OF
PEOPLE.

It's a shame when you get lost in a project, or go out on a tour, or get stuck in
a demanding relationship, and find out that
all of your old contacts have dried up.

You go to call a booking agent you used to
see weekly, and she says, "I'm sorry - I
don't really remember you. You're going to
have to remind me ... "

A successful publicist advises that you
secretly give everyone in your phonebook
an A, B, C, D, E, or F. That's your A-list
(call every 3 weeks), B-list, (every 5
weeks), C-list (every few months), D-list
(twice a year), and Friends.

There are a few people in my life that would have disappeared long ago if they hadn't been so persistent in calling me every month, or insisting on a face-to-face a couple times a year.

Go through your database, and call those people just to say, "Hi." Or - even better - know their interests and life (from memory or perhaps from your notes) - and call them with some news that's of interest to them, even if it's of no other interest to you.

In other words, don't *only* call to say "How are you?" when it's always going to end with "So - can you come to my gig tomorrow night?" Call unselfishly. Call with some news that will make them happy. Keep in touch to make both of your lives better.

DATABASE TIPS.

Database tips, from an expert:

- Best programs, in order: (1) Indie Band Manager: *http://www.IndieBandManager.com*. It does EVERYTHING I recommend. It works on Mac and Windows. And it's only $39. If you don't have a database program already, start with that. (2) Filemaker Pro. Sells for $299 but you can find it used on EBay.com for $40. Both Mac and Windows. Totally flexible. (3) MS Works or Claris Works comes with a database section. These programs are usually free and included on your computer. (4) ACT. *http://www.act.com* Sells for $189. ACT is meant more as a "salesman's tool" and so it's more corporate, and less flexible. But it is already set up to do exactly what you want. On the Mac, I've heard that "Now Contact Manager" is very similar to Act. (5) MS Access. It's like using an army tank to go do your groceries. It's so powerful and complicated that it might take you a long time to learn. But like Filemaker, it can do everything you need if you harness it. (6) MS Outlook. Yuk. Inflexible. Hit by viruses. But if you have it already and you can't afford something new, go with it. (7) Do NOT use a spreadsheet like MS Excel, or a word processor, or a notebook of paper. These just won't do the job. Choose from #1-#5.

- Keywords! Multiple keywords are the most important thing in your database. Every person in your address book should have a few words attached to their record like "drums, web design, percussion" or "agent, club owner, songwriter". Some folks will

only have one word there, some will have
a list of the 25 instruments they can
play. This comes in the most handy when
you need to find "drums" in Texas, or
you're trying to remember the full name of
that web designer named "Dave". If your
address book program doesn't have keywords
already, put it in there! Find out how!
It'll save your life many times.

- Collect all the information you can.
Have areas in your database program for
first name, last name, two phone numbers,
fax, email, website (know their website!),
two address lines, country, keywords (see
above), mailing list tags (who gets your
mailings and who doesn't want them), date
last contacted, and very important: NOTES.
Other ideas would be birthday, interests,
and referred by (or "met through").

- NOTES should be a big giant text area
underneath their contact info, where
you're free to type type type anything you
want. Type notes from your conversations.
Cut-and-paste Emails they've sent you. In
ACT and Filemaker you can set it up to make
an "event" for every single conversation or
contact you have, each with its own notes.
Very handy. Set this up if you can. But
even if you do, keep the big giant Notes

field for all permanent notes you want to remember about this person.

- Learn how to mail-merge these people, so you can send them all a personalized Email or letter. Using a person's name in the letter instead of "Dear Music Industry Professional".

MEET THREE NEW PEOPLE EVERY WEEK.

One of the best books about the music business was called "Making It in the New Music Business" by James Riordan.

He suggested that, as an aspiring musician (or producer/agent/writer/etc.) - you make a point to meet three new people in the music industry every week. (And, as he says, not just burned-out guitarists.)

Imagine that! Three new people every single week—people that could actually help your career! In a year from now you'll have relationships with over 150 new people that are potential "lottery tickets" - and hopefully the interest is mutual. (Meaning - always keep in mind how YOU can help someone, not just how they can help you.)

The thing is, you have to *develop* these relationships. Put them on your A, B, or

C list. Stay in touch. Go beyond the introduction, and really get to know these people, what they're looking for in business and life, what they're interested in, and how you can help them.

ALWAYS THINK HOW YOU CAN HELP SOMEONE.

As you're meeting all of these people in your life and career, always keep in mind how you can help someone. You should practically meditate on it before contacting them.

There must be someone you know that is exactly what they're looking for. There must be some resource you've got that would really make their day. Some favor you can do.

An article you read in this morning's paper might be of particular interest to someone you met last summer. Cut it out and mail it to them. A film/TV music supervisor might mention she's getting married and is looking for a reggae band. You don't do reggae, but with your database you can help her find a great band that does.

Maybe you spent 3 months shopping for a laptop. Maybe a booking agent you met

today mentioned that he's looking for a
new laptop. Send him a fax or Email with
all the best info you found.

Give give give, and sometimes you will
receive.

GET PERSONAL.

Some people, out of the thousands I know,
actually contact me on a regular basis. I
consider them friends.

But some of those always stick with a
strict business "script" when they call:
"Hi I'm calling to check in to see how
sales are doing, if you need more inventory, how things are going."

Others seem to have the gift of Smalltalk.
I don't know how they do it, but soon
we're talking about my girlfriend, their
dogs, about yoga, high school, Japan, and
something that happened on the way to work
today.

Now—when an opportunity comes up to help
someone - (say, a Film/TV person I know
calls up and asks "who's good in that standard rock genre?") - guess who comes to
mind first?

The person who hasn't departed from the standard business call, or the person who went beyond?

Be a real person. Be a friend.

Don't always be selling yourself. You'll be like that annoying uncle who shows up at the family reunion to try to sell everyone on life insurance.

Have the confidence to know that being a cool person, being a friend, will sell you more than being a pushy salesperson.

People do business with people they like. With their friends, whenever possible.

DON'T BE AFRAID TO ASK FOR FAVORS.

Don't be afraid to ask for favors.

Some people LIKE doing favors.

It's like asking for directions in New York city. People's egos get stroked when they know the answer to something you're asking. They'll gladly answer to show off their knowledge.

One bold musician I know called me up one day and said, "I'm coming to New York in 2 months. Can you give me a list of all the important contacts you think I should meet?" What guts! But I laughed, and did a search in my database, Emailing him a list of 40 people he should call, and mention my name.

Sometimes you need to find something specific: a video director for cheap, a PA system you can borrow for a month, a free rehearsal studio. Call up everyone you know and ask! This network of friends you are creating will have everything you want in life.

Some rare and lucky folks (perhaps on your "band mailing list") have time on their hands and would rather help you do something, than sit at home in front of the TV another night. Need help doing flyers? Help getting equipment to a show? Go ahead and ask!

KEEP IN TOUCH!

Mentioned earlier, but important enough to say again.

Sometimes the difference between success and failure is just a matter of keeping in touch!

There are some AMAZING musicians who have sent a CD to CD Baby, and when I heard it, I flipped. In a few cases, I've stopped what I was doing at that moment, picked up the phone and called them wherever they were to tell them I thought they were a total genius. (Believe me - this is rare. Maybe 1 in 500 CDs that I hear.)

Often I get an answering machine, and guess what... they don't call back!! What masochistic anti-social success-sabotaging kind of thing is that to do?

Then 2 weeks later I've forgotten about their CD as new ones came in.

The lesson: If they would have just called back, and kept in touch, they may have a fan like no other at the head of one of the largest distributors of independent music on the web. A fan that would go out on a limb to help their career in ways others just dream of. But they never kept in touch and now I can't remember their names.

Some others whose CDs didn't really catch my attention the first time around, just keep in touch so well that I often find myself helping them more as a friend than a fan.

Keep in touch, keep in touch, keep in touch!

People forget you very fast.

SMALL GIFTS GO A LONG WAY.

10 years ago, I worked at Warner/Chappell Music Publishing. Being the largest music publisher in the world, I dealt with thousands of songwriters. Most of them I can't remember their names.0

James Maestro, a great songwriter from Hoboken, got me a cool little "Mother Mary" keychain when he was touring in Spain.

Gerry DeVeaux, a successful R&B/dance songwriter, got me some funky plastic fish with lights inside, like Christmas ornaments, when he went to the Bahamas.

And Jane Kelly Williams got me a red sweatshirt from the Gap, for helping her out with a demo session. I was thrilled.

Can you believe I remember these details 10 years later? Believe it!

A little gift you might give to someone, as you climb the ladder of success, may go

a long long way, and mean a lot to someone down the road.

If any of the three people above called me
today to ask a favor, you can be sure I'd
stop what I was doing to help them out.

Be generous. It will be returned. As you
stay in the music biz, you're going to see
the same faces for years to come.

[P.S. Don't send ME gifts! You've already
got my attention. Use this technique on
other people.]

KEEP IN TOUCH—(LONG VERSION).

Give away lots of CDs. But do NOT just
toss them away. Make every one count!!

Get volunteer friends/bandmembers/fans to
help call or Email and track the results
of as many of these as possible.

Go ahead and ask for favors - be a little
bit of a pest. Ask each mag what they'd
want to put you on the cover. Take notes
of each conversation.

Keep everyone happy. Don't lose touch. Ask
for references. Ask if there's anyone else
they know that can help you. Then contact
all THOSE people, and keep doing it.

It's a LOT of Emailing and calling. But it means EVERYTHING. (As long as you super-humanly balance this with making new music and writing great songs.)

I think KEEPING IN TOUCH is THE single most important thing. Here's why:

Whenever I'm talking to someone in the "industry" or have the opportunity to help promote a CD Baby member, I often find myself hooking up the person who I just got off the phone with. (You know - "Oh I was just talking with Scott from the band called the Rosenbergs, you should talk to them - he's home right now, and just told me how well their tour is going!")

On the flip side, there are 60 people a week or so who submit their CD to CD Baby, I put it in the store, I email them but they never reply, I send them checks for CDs sold but never hear from them.

I often wonder who these people are that just let a potential fruitful relationship just disappear into anonymity.

(Do I sell a band called Conundrum? Umm ... let me check the database. Well it says here I do. I don't know them, though.) And CD Baby is just ONE company!

Imagine if you actually stayed "close" with 100 little companies! Or 1000!! You'd have people in all corners of the industry everywhere constantly recommending you, referring you, hooking you up with opportunities, promoting you, etc. You'd be very successful, very soon.

When you're on tour, look up all the people who you've sent CDs to in that area. Meet with them. Sleep at their house.

Ask everyone's advice. Pick everyone's brain. Hear their thoughts & point of view. Remember it.

Oh, send them a present every now and then. Chad the Dungeon Bunny sent me a bag of Baby Ruths. Guess who comes to mind first now when people are asking for his kind of music??

God know that I think of it I probably remember every little present anyone has ever given me in my 10 years being in the music biz. I can count them one hand. It's such a rare wonderful surprise.

On the flip side, I made a friend for life at the top ranks of BMI because I showed up to his office with a pizza for our meeting. (Luckily he was hungry and never forgot it.)

Radio stations are just people. Magazines are just people. Websites are just people. Record companies are just people.

People like to work with their FRIENDS whenever possible. Be a good friend. Be a real person, not a slick schmoozer. If you're acting TOO professional in all this "keeping in touch" then it just sounds fake and will be forgotten.

Oh, and try to sense when they don't like you. Sometimes they just don't like your music, and aren't willing to help. Don't take it personally. Mark it in your address book/database and move on to the next.

LIFE IS LIKE HIGH SCHOOL.

Last week a musician wrote an Email to the effect of, "I've been working hard - why isn't it paying off?"

Keep this in mind ... LIFE IS LIKE HIGH SCHOOL.

When you're in High School, it's ALL about popularity, clicks, being 'cool', what you wear, what parties you're at, etc.

When you go to College, the focus shifts to academic achievement.

Many people get out of college thinking the world will be like that. "The harder you work, the more you should be rewarded." - But it's not.

Life is like High School. It's all about who you know, how socially charming you are, what 'scene' you're in, what you wear, what parties you're at, flirting, and -being 'cool'.

BUT YOU CAN MAKE THIS WORK IN YOUR FAVOR.

When I think about every big leap that happened in my career, it was always because of "someone I knew." Always friends of friends. People in some position of power who I kept in touch with, did favors for, and got the same in return.

Go meet 3 people each week you think could help your career. Be a good friend. Make it mutually beneficial, not some suck-up relationship. There's always some resource you have that can totally help out someone who may be "above" you on the ladder. Invite a NEW friend to a party or show you know about.

For years I was booked solid, touring the college market, making way too much $$, not because I'm GOOD, but because we made a FUN, ENTERTAINING, "COOL" show. We won the popularity contest in a sense.

I think it's possible to approach the music business as if you were a new kid going to a new high school, and wanted to be the most popular kid in class. Sounds shallow, but it works.

Ask Andy Warhol, or someone like Prince who actually made GREAT music, but knew how to toss in a little controversy & sex appeal to get the world's attention.

MAKE THESE HABITS, AND THEY WON'T SEEM HARD.

All of these suggestions may sound exhausting to you.

But keep that database at your fingertips. Get used to taking 1 minute after a conversation to take some notes about it. Give some of these ideas a try.

You can probably tell, by reading this, that if you were to actually DO all of these things mentioned, you'd be much more successful than you are now. The gates of life would swing wide open.

Hard to start, but easy to continue.

Incredibly powerful when done every day. (Like a little river made the Grand Canyon.)

Make these habits, and they won't seem hard.

SHINING EXAMPLE: RAYKO.

I went to the Eat'm Music Conference in Las Vegas, summer 1999. Hundreds of artists there but, one made the biggest impression on me. I noticed her first because she's gorgeous, but the other stuff quickly made that unimportant - and there's an inspiring lesson in here.

Her name is Rayko. Japanese musician from L.A. *http://www.cdbaby.com/rayko http://www.rayko.com*

She was going up to every single person at the conference introducing herself, getting into great conversations, finding out what everyone does, taking notes. Every time someone handed her a business card, she grabbed her pen and wrote down notes about that person on the back, to help her remember.

She probably befriended hundreds of people in 3 days, including me.

Whenever she has a show on the road, she goes in the day before to do countless meet-and-greet interviews, in-store appearances, flyer-promotion, and every other promotion tool you've ever heard of. She gets right into the crowd after every show to sell CDs and sign up hundreds of people to the mailing list.

She answers every fan letter with a hand-written letter. She immediately sends a thank-you card to every biz contact she meets.

And all the while, she's constantly prac-ticing and writing and recording new music.

I was on the receiving end of this when, the very first day back from the confer-ence, she called me in New York to take care of getting on to CD Baby. Who knows if she called 200 people that day, but damn she knows how to make you feel like you're the most important one. (And yep - 2 days later her whole package with CDs, shirts, videos, and purple handwritten letter were at my door.)

This is exactly the same success story I've heard is behind Garth Brooks and Madonna (and even Bill Clinton, actually.)

Meeting everyone. Remembering everyone's name. Developing relationships. Following up and constantly keeping in touch. Treating everyone special.

Who knows if this is just part of her personality, or if it's a trait she developed because her career is THAT important to her.

So—the real point of giving you all these details - is analyzing your own networking and promoting efforts. I've heard many great records at CD Baby. But I've only seen a few great promoters.

Maybe there are people out there promoting their butts off and I just don't know about it - the same way I wouldn't have known about Rayko if I wasn't in that room at that moment.

If you care about your music, and you really REALLY want - in your heart and bones - to become incredibly successful at it, you're going to have to go meet tons of people and "plug away" with tireless drive, and joyful determination every waking moment.

Meet every person you can and treat them the way you'd love to be treated.

And still somehow balance this with making the best music you can and constantly improving your songwriting and performing skills.

######### THE POWER OF WORDS #########
Derek Sivers - *http://www.cdbaby.net/derek*

ON THE INTERNET, WORDS MATTER MORE THAN EVER.

On the radio, descriptions don't matter. People hear your song one time or a hundred times, they decide they like it, and hopefully the DJ says who it is.

In concert, descriptions don't matter. You don't have to describe your music while you're performing. You get on stage and perform. People love it, or like it, or they don't. No words necessary.

But on the internet, and in print, and in conversation, words matter a LOT.

If you take just one night to come up with some good descriptions of your music, you can use those phrases for years, and you will find many MANY more fans than you will without descriptions.

On the internet, whether web or Email, you need to entice people to click their mouse before they'll ever become a fan.

In order to get someone to listen to your sound clips, sign your mailing list, or buy your CD, you have to: (1) catch their attention (2) appeal to their senses or emotions (3) arouse their curiosity (4) persuade them to do something about it (click!)

A SHORT DESCRIPTION - 10 SECONDS OR LESS

Most of the world has never heard your music.

Most of the world WON'T hear your music, unless you do a good job describing it.

It's like a Hollywood screenplay. You not only have to write a great screenplay, but you have to have a great description of it that you can say in 10 seconds or less, in order to catch people's attention.

Find a way to describe your music that would catch anyone's attention, AND describe it accurately. No use coming up with a funny description of your music if it doesn't actually describe what you really sound like!

HOW TO GET THE BEST SHORT DESCRIPTION OF YOUR MUSIC:

(1) Ask friends for their opinion. Ask a friend who talks too much, or someone in sales, to tell someone about you. Listen in, and remember. (2) Get silly. Get drunk. Write down 50 ridiculous descriptions with some drunk friends. One of them may be good. (3) Take your favorite one and test it on the world. Whenever you meet strangers, and they ask about your music, have your catch phrase handy. If it doesn't make their eyebrows go up, try a different one. (4) Send an Email to everyone on your Emailing list. Give them your three favorite phrases and let them pick which they like the best. Let them offer a better one.

Once you've got a great one, you'll know it.

Keep using it again and again until people almost associate your name with that one-sentence-phrase that describes it beautifully and accurately.

THINK LIKE A PERSON OR POET, NOT A MUSICIAN.

When describing your music, PLEASE don't be a musician.

Don't say, "The wonderful harmonies and arrangements on this release are sure to delight! Not to mention the tight rhythm section and insightful lyrics!"

Real people don't think like that.

Think what one teenager down at the mall would say to another, when describing what they love about your CD.

("Dude - it's like if Korn hadn't wimped out. It's like Busta Rhymes went metal, but they're from Mars or somethin. It's slammin. And you gotta see that picture on the inside cover!")

Think what an office-worker who wasn't much a music expert would say to a friend about your music.

("It's cute! They have this song that has a little "hoop-hoop!" at the beginning, with that baby voice. It's kinda funky! And he's got this sexy bedroom voice. Funny video.")

Real people often compare an artist to other famous artists. Real people talk about the overall "vibe" or sound of something.

Real people DON'T talk about "insightful lyrics" and "wonderful harmonies" and "tight musicianship". That's musician-speak. (OK - *some* music fans are deep enough into music that they do end up using these musician terms. But that's pretty rare.)

Play your music for some non-musicians, and ask them what they'd say to a friend about it.

Learn to describe your music in ways that actually *reach* people's emotion and imagination, and your music itself will be that much more likely to reach and touch people.

Your descriptions of your music should be almost as exciting (or touching, or sad, or shocking) as the music itself.

READ ABOUT NEW MUSIC. USE THE TRICKS THAT WORKED ON YOU.

Go get a magazine like CMJ, or Magnet, or Alternative Press.

You'll read about (and see pictures of) dozens of artists who you've never heard of before.

Out of that whole magazine, only one or two will really catch your attention.

WHY?

I don't have the answer. Only you do. Ask yourself why a certain headline or photo or article caught your attention.

(Was it something about the opening sentence? Was it a curious tidbit about the background of the singer? What was it exactly that intrigued you?)

Analyze that. Use that. Adapt those techniques to try writing a headline or article about your music.

YES YOU DO SOUND LIKE SOMETHING OR SOMEONE.

Yes you DO sound like something or someone.

Thousands of musicians describe themselves as sounding "Totally unique. There is nothing like this music you have ever heard!" Then when you put on the CD, it's straight-up pop/rock/blues. Instant disappointment.

When asked, many musicians think it's fine to say, "We don't sound like anyone." Or when asked what kind of music they play, say, "You can't describe it. Just check it out."

That's just lazy, inconsiderate, and stupid.

What if a business out in New Jersey somewhere said, "We can't describe what our
store does. Just check it out!" Would
you get in your car and spend a Saturday
driving out to Route 17 to check it out?
No!

You have to convince people! Grab their
curiosity. Describe what you actually do,
in an interesting way!

Make the wheels in their head turn. Make
them taste it, hear it, see it, want it.

Be accurate, and don't disappoint. Read
that twice: (1) - Be accurate. (2) - Don't
disappoint.

This is a creative writing exercise. You
can do it. It's important. It will make
the right people stop and listen to your
music.

BLAH BLAH BLAH ... WHAT NOT TO SAY.

At CD Baby we ask musicians to give a one-
sentence description of their style. You'd
be surprised how many artists say, "A
great 4-piece band from North Carolina.
A hot new artist for the new millennium.
A band you're sure to enjoy!"

Imagine if you ran into an old friend who now owned his own business, and you asked what his company does. Then he says, "We're a top-notch 9-person company in New Jersey. We believe in service, quality, and dependability."

-= yawn =-

Would you remember that 1 minute later or give a damn what that business did?

Nope. They lost you.

Think how many people you're losing when you describe your music in a boring, or generic way.

When asked for a little more info, musicians often say "The members grew up in Boston and met in high school. After the bassist left to pursue another career, they found a replacement who has solidified the lineup as it stands today. They regularly play the local club scene."

Imagine a computer store saying, "Our VP of finance graduated from Penn State. We found our office manager through an employment agency. After our initial marketing director left ... "

-= yawn =-

When a fan is learning about an artist for the first time, the last thing they care about is uneventful band history. As a rule, it's safe to assume people don't care about your history until you've got a gold record. Don't bore them with it before then. (Unless it's buried deep in your website for those few folks that are deeply curious.)

Describe your music or history in a way that you would want a total stranger running a little shop somewhere to describe his business to you.

OR YOU CAN NOT TALK AT ALL

Words got you down? Nothing new to say?

Then spend some money on a great photographer.

Calvin Klein showed you don't have to talk and talk and talk.

But if you don't, it's ALLLLL up to the image.

Unless you're in heavy rotation on top 40 radio stations, it's not very easy for people to hear your music. They have to go seek you out, and make an effort to go hear you.

Music is like perfume. You have to con-vince and persuade people, with your words and images, to take that initiative, to make an effort, to hear your music.

If you try to just "let the music speak for itself" most people will never hear you.

HAVE FUN - DO NOT BE CORPORATE

Never use corporate marketing-speak.

Be weird.

Be a real person.

Sound like one person speaking to one person.

This is a big reason why it's COOL to be indie instead of corporate.

Real people respond better to the weird fun stuff.

######### TOOLS AND WEAPONS #########
Derek Sivers - *http://www.cdbaby.net/derek*

PROMO BOX ON YOUR DESKTOP

The self-promoting musician of the past needed to always have a presskit (with CD and photo) nearby and ready to send.

The modern self-promoting musician needs to keep a "PROMO BOX" folder on the desktop of your computer.

It will take you just one hour to put together, and you'll be able to use it again and again and again:

MAKE A FOLDER ON YOUR DESKTOP CALLED "PROMO BOX" (or something) AND PUT THESE THINGS INSIDE FOR QUICK EASY ACCESS:

1. At least one full-length MP3 file of a track from your CD. Encoded at the standard 128k bitrate. Give it a nice long name, without spaces, so that if anyone runs across it on the web they know who it is. (Example: RACHAEL_SAGE-sister-song.mp3) Preferably have 3-5 songs from your CD encoded here, ready to go.
2. An entertaining bio written four times, in four different lengths. - Long long version (over 3 paragraphs. 1-2 pages. exhaustive and rarely used.) - Medium long version (2–4 entertaining and important paragraphs. The top end of what people will sit and read on the web.) - Short version (1 killer paragraph) - One-liner (1 killer sentence)
3. Quotes from reviews: - one big text file with every review you've ever

gotten, all typed out and credited - one text file with just the best short quotes from these reviews

4. Graphics, with a few different sizes of each: - artist photos (studio shot, live shot, up close, far away) - album cover graphic (big version, small version) - your logo, if you have one

IF YOU DO THIS, JUST ONCE, then the job of uploading your information to another website will be painless. You'll just say, "da-da-da! all done!" and let your MP3s upload while you go make dinner.

KNOW THE IMPORTANT SKILLS

Like proper manners, or knowing how to drive, here are some things in the online world you just need to know:

1. EMAIL - Have a good signature file that tells who you are, how to find you, and entices people to click through to your web address. All in 4 lines or less. - How to make good subject headers. So when your Email is one of 500 in an "IN" box, it will say exactly what is contained inside, from the other person's point of view. - How to quote someone's

email message back to them. Or not. - How to subscribe to, post messages to, and unsubscribe from to a mailing list. - Manners. Spelling. Punctuation. How to turn off your caps lock key, and not use 25 exclamation points in a row. - How to communicate personality through these typewriter keys. - Separate sentences into paragraphs. Reading a computer screen is different from reading a book. There's no paper to waste - leave plenty of space.

2. DATABASE SKILLS - Know how to work your "address book" program. How to find people, sort, print, add, remove, change, and do bigger find commands (how to find all guitarists in the 818 area code) - Keep it nice and clean and updated. Keep street address separated from the city, state, zip, country. Don't be sloppy in these early stages. - Assume you ARE going to get more popular and soon your little address book will need to sort thousands of people. - If you get really fancy, track each contact you have with someone: each call, email, visit. It comes in handy when someone from a year ago calls you up saying, "It's George! Remember?"

3. WEB SKILLS - Get comfortable uploading an Mp3 file. (Practice at mp3.com, iuma.com, rollingstone.com) - Sort your bookmarks/favorites into categories/folders so you can find things later.

YOUR INTERACTIVE WEBSITE

Your website can be your best tool, if you MAKE IT COMMUNICATE **WITH** YOUR FANS and potential fans, TWO-WAY.

Your website should get people involve, make them want to introduce themselves, ask questions, shout out.

YOUR WEBSITE SHOULD:

#1 - Get their Email address! Interact! Make an easy fill-out form.

(hint: try a fun question like "who are you?" or "do you know your own name?")

#2 - Encourage them to buy your CD, constantly. It's a great way to start a relationship.

#3 - Show what's unique about you. Image, quirks, colors, moods.

#4 - Make the sound clips easy to get to, not buried under layers

#5 - Answer the obvious questions: who are you, what do you look like, let me hear the music

#6 - Acknowledge them! Have their pictures on your site. Answer their questions on your site. Show them they ARE a part of your life.

The best webhosting company to host musicians' websites, and help you do the hard stuff is Hostbaby! http://www.hostbaby.com

The web has replaced college radio as THE way to turn people on to your music.

Use it!

PLEASE FORWARD THIS EMAIL TO EVERY MUSICIAN YOU THINK DESERVES MORE ATTENTION

Copyright 2003, Derek Sivers, CD Baby
http://www.cdbaby.com <--- store to sell your CDs
http://www.cdbaby.net <--- tips for musicians
http://www.cdbaby.org <--- news, opportunities, etc.

RECOMMENDED BOOKS:

GUERRILLA P.R. - by Michael Levine (the best book I've ever read about getting attention)

*http://www.amazon.com/exec/obidos/ASIN/
0887306640/cdbaby*

GUERRILLA MARKETING EXCELLENCE - by Jay
Conrad Levinson (very concrete do-able
tips on marketing your music)
*http:// www.amazon.com/exec/obidos/ASIN/
0395608449/cdbaby*

SELLING THE INVISIBLE - by Harry Beckwith
(an amazing marketing book. my biggest
inspiration for the tips, above.)
*http:// www.amazon.com/exec/obidos/ASIN/
0446520942/ cdbaby*

THINK AND GROW RICH - by Napoleon Hill
(replace the word "money" with "talent" and
it's a classic book about being a great
musician.)
*http://www.amazon.com/exec/obidos/ASIN/
0449214923/cdbaby*

CONCERT PROMOTER INTERVIEWS:

The following excerpt of text is from the book, *Making the Show Go*, a work in progress by Conrad E. Muller and Nora Percival Muller.

Who is the Promoter or Producer, and What Does a Producer Do?

The promoter finds the money, the act, and the hall. The promoter usually also hires the crew, although some performers and halls have their own crews. Most professional crews and performers expect to be paid at the show (or before it), and the promoter needs to be ready for this. Once the production is under way, the promoter has three primary jobs: keeping the show on schedule; keeping the show within budget (good luck!); and keeping everyone working together smoothly. The best way to ensure a happy crew is to see that everyone feels appreciated.

Choosing an act

- Many people will already have an act picked out when they decide to produce a show. If you do not have a specific act in mind and you are looking for one, try to choose a performer or group you like. The first time you produce a show will require extra energy, and it will help if you are really looking forward to the show.
- When possible, choose an act which is already performing near your area. This will keep transportation costs down, and it may help you negotiate a lower performance fee.
- Most of the time you will book your act through an agent. Whether you work through an agent or directly with the performers, be sure you get everything in writing. Often you must do a lot of business over the phone. Make sure you and the performers' representative agree that nothing is final until you both have it in writing and signed. Sometimes last minute changes must be made by phone, on faith, but they are likely to be less of a problem if they are based on solid signed contracts. Refer to the appendix for more about contracts.

- When should you book an act? Most promoters and performers like to set dates months, even a year, in advance of the show. Sometimes you hear of an opportunity at the last minute. By all means, consider serendipitous offerings, but be sure to allow enough time to get the show together, and most important, give yourself time for effective publicity. Choosing a date and time.
- It's hard to give advice on the proper season to have a concert. A well publicized show featuring a popular act could do well almost any time. If the weather can be expected to be good, an outdoor or tent show could be just the ticket to draw an out-of-season crowd. For a typical concert by a typical act, try to choose a date in the fall or spring, well away from holidays and potentially bad driving weather.
- If other promoters have shows on the same date as yours, they might draw some of your customers away. Check with local agencies who keep track of community events (such as arts councils) to find uncrowded dates. Be sure to announce your show soon enough and prominently enough to allow others to avoid schedule conflicts.
- Most events are schedule for the early evening, starting late enough that people can get there after work, and ending early enough that people can get to sleep in time to get up for work the next day. Friday and Saturday evening events often run a little later than mid-week ones, and events geared to special audiences (such as children) should, of course, be timed to coincide with the target audiences needs.

Choosing a venue

- Availability: Can you rent it on the dates when you need it?
- Capacity of the house: Try to predict the size of the audience. This depends on many factors, including weather, "draw" of the act (how popular it is in your area), how much advertising you do, the ticket price, and competing events going on simultaneously (including other shows, family holidays such as Christmas and Easter, and sporting events. Accurately predicting the size of the audience is difficult, even for experienced promoters, and it takes a bit of luck, along with lots of information, to make a reasonable guess. Find out how big the crowds have been at the act's last few shows in towns in your area.
- Location: Is the venue well known or easy to find? Is it close to the center of population?
- Security: Will the people, equipment, vehicles, etc. be safe? Can you control who gets in?
- Parking: Is there enough parking? Will the cars be safe? Will it be convenient and safe for the crew and audience to get into the hall?
- Stage size: Is the stage big enough but not too big?
- Sound and acoustics: How will it sound? How big a sound system will be necessary? Will it sound good everywhere? Is there enough electrical power available for the required sound system? Is there a house sound system you can use?
- Lights: Are there lighting instruments available? Is there a dimmer board? How many channels? Are there

enough circuits to carry the number of lights you want to use? Does the wiring look safe? Are the outlets conveniently located? Are there places to hang lights?

- View (sight lines): How is the view from the corners and back of the house?
- Other facilities and equipment available at the hall: Dressing rooms? Stage platforms? Chairs? Locked storage? Kitchen? Loading dock?
- Price: How much will you be charged to use it? The chairs, stage platforms, dressing rooms, kitchen, and equipment may cost extra. Be sure to ask.

Publicity

- Publicity is the promoter's responsibility. Professional acts will be able to provide you with promotional materials. They should do this automatically, but they may forget, in which case you must remind them. Be sure to get promotional materials, as well as posters, soon enough to be able to use them effectively.
- When to advertise: The following timetable was developed for use in small cities. Four to six weeks before the show, contact monthly publications which have events calendars for your area. This is also the time to announce the show in publications outside your local area, giving people who will have to come a significant distance time to make plans. Two weeks before the show, put up the posters and start to push your show into the local media. If people know a group they want to see is coming, they will rearrange their schedules to

come to the show, if they have enough warning. So if you are promoting a show with a well-known act and want a big crowd, you may want to begin to advertise sooner. In any case, save the big promotional push for the last two weeks to keep the excitement up and draw in the people who are undecided.

- Posters are sometimes provided by the act, in which case all you have to do is add the date, time, location, ticket price, and promoter's name at the bottom. Find out if the posters are included in the performers' fee, and be sure you are going to get enough for every location you want to cover. Posters can also be designed and printed locally. You will need to have a photo or art work, and you will need to typeset the text. The traditional way is to use press-on letters and paste on the graphics to make your original, or have a printer do it for you. These days most people use computers. We often desk-top publish two sizes of posters. For large posters (usually 11"×17"), we use desk-top publishing for the text, which we then paste up with graphics and give to a copy shop for printing. These go up in locations where there is enough space for them. Smaller ones (8.5"×11"), which are all that some stores and bulletin boards will let you put up, can be made completely on the computer, using generic graphics, or can also be printed at a copy shop, using a reduction of the large poster. Make extra posters. You will often find a few extra places to hang them, and sometimes they will get pulled down or defaced, and you will have to replace them.

- Radio advertising is effective and not too expensive. Ask about special package prices. TV advertising is usually too expensive for small shows, and not noticeably more effective than radio. Some cable systems have inexpensive advertising space on a bulletin board channel. If the sponsor is a non-profit organization, local public radio stations may give you some spots. Even commercial radio stations sometimes will let non-profits use their community announcements program. Also, try to arrange a live radio interview with the main performer on the day before or the day of the event. These can be done in the studio, if the performer is already in town, or can be done by phone from wherever the performer happens to be. They are most often possible on public radio stations.
- Daily newspaper advertising can be a good investment if you can afford an ad that is big enough to catch people's attention. Weekly newspapers often provide a better cost/benefit ratio. Check out the smaller and special purpose papers in your area.
- Announcing your show at other events can be effective, if you can arrange it.
- Magazines and seasonal publications can be a good way to reach people if your show is planned far enough in advance (and you have the money and a good looking ad). A display ad in the sponsoring organization's newsletter should be free and can be very effective.
- Direct mail is usually expensive and not usually effective, but you might want to do a direct mailing if you have a mailing list that looks like it has a lot of names of people who would come to your show.

Ticket sales

- How much to charge for tickets: Price the tickets about the same as similar shows in your area.
- Where to sell tickets: Make sure it is easy for people to buy tickets. Find conveniently located places that will sell tickets for you. These might include book stores, regular ticket outlets, and the sponsor's location(s). Stores that don't usually sell tickets may be willing to sell them for you to get people into the store or to help your sponsoring organization.
- When to sell tickets: Tickets should go on sale when the ads appear in the papers and the posters go up (about two weeks before the event). If you begin to advertise before tickets are available, be sure to include in your ads the date tickets will go on sale.
- The tickets should be attractive, distinctive, and of a reasonable size. They should be printed on good-quality paper, so they will still be in one piece after being carried in a wallet for a couple of weeks. Graphics are nice, but not if they make the text too small to read. It is easy to print tickets on a computer with a word-processing program. Print multiple tickets on heavy, colored paper and cut them out yourself, or print up one sheet of tickets and have a copy shop print them on colored card stock and cut them out.
- Treat tickets like money, because that's what they are. Number all the tickets and keep track of who has them. Tickets can be numbered by some printing companies or with a special, self-inking hand stamp that advances

206 THE MUSICIAN'S AND SINGER'S SURVIVAL GUIDE

one digit each time you stamp with it. Ours is a Cascade Numbering Machine M4-C327. Most office supply stores have stamps similar to these or can get them.

Budgeting

- Once you have estimated ticket sales, set a ticket price, and tentatively chosen a hall, you're ready to develop a budget. This will tell you if you can proceed with your event as planned or if you need to drop back and try another approach.

- Expected income: You have the potential to make money from ticket sales, refreshment sales, and sales of posters, tapes/CDs, and tee-shirts. Performers usually get most or all of the money for tapes and CDs, especially at small concerts. At large concerts, the house often takes a percentage, and in all cases, there is sales tax.

- Expected expenses: You may have to spend money on any or all of the following: performers' fee or percentage; performers' expenses; your personal expenses (meals, transportation, etc.); advertising; cost of printing, distributing, and selling tickets; production costs, including hall rental, security and front-of-house staff (ushers, box office, ticket takers), equipment rental (sound equipment, lighting equipment, stage platforms, chairs, barricades, etc.), and crew wages and expenses; costs of selling refreshments, including food and/or drinks, ice and condiments, serving supplies (cups, plates, forks, spoons, napkins, warmer fuel, etc.), clean up supplies (soap, paper towels, trash can liners, etc.), equipment (coolers, warmers, tappers, tables, chairs, cash register or cash box, trash cans, mops, brooms, etc.), and wages; taxes, permits, bonds, and insurance; and contingency funds.

- You will need change for both the ticket sales and concessions. Don't forget that you may have to make rental deposits on the hall and equipment. You also might have to make damage deposits.

- Plan to keep close track of everything you earn and spend. Ideally, you should use a spreadsheet, listing the budgeted amount at the top of each income and expense category column. As you collect money and pay expenses, record it in the appropriate column. When the show is over, you will know how much you made and spent, and how close you came to your budget estimates. This information will be extremely valuable when you do your next show.

Hospitality for the performers is the promoter's responsibility. Usually, the act will let you know what they expect in the way of refreshments. This is often negotiable, so if their requests seem unreasonable or difficult, don't just quietly accept them.

Stage passes and complimentary tickets are ultimately the promoter's responsibility, though the box office manager may be able to actually give out the comp tickets.

An Interview with Ricci Terranova of all in Black productions, a Small Concert Promotion Company Based in Thousand Oaks, California.

TELL US A LITTLE ABOUT YOURSELF AND YOUR COMPANY

ALL IN BLACK is mainly a production company, though we also book and promote as well ... our main thing is finding ideas for shows that excite us and then producing it ourselves ... we secure the venue, the talent and then help with the overall promotion of the show. In the future we would love to be involved with management and possibly have our own label. The main objective of ALL IN BLACK is to produce good quality shows and most importantly take good care of the bands and let them know they are appreciated.

WHAT IS THE CURRENT STATE OF THE MUSIC BUSINESS WITH REGARD TO GETTING LOCAL PAYING GIGS?

Unfortunately "pay to play" and "preselling" of tickets have become the norm. Personally I think it's wrong to have a band "volunteer" their talent while others profit. I can't speak for others, but ALL IN BLACK pays all our artists even if you are a local high school band.

WHAT TYPE OF ACTS ARE MOST IN DEMAND?

Well if we are booking for our local shows, we look for local original bands that will fit well on the bill. We also look for original bands from outside the immediate area that we feel will be a "natural fit" so that we can hopefully get them exposure to a new audience. For corporate or city sponsored gigs such as "Concerts In The Park" the demand is more for safe cover bands, world music, Latin bands and occasionally a safe tribute band. They tend to stay away from something that's too edgy because these tend to be more of a family type atmosphere. From our experience with working with special events coordinators, they look for bands that really know how to entertain their crowd and get them involved. That will score big points with them and possibly lead to repeat appearances. Casino buyers usually call us for classic rock and roll tribute bands.

HOW SHOULD MUSICIANS APPROACH THE GIG MARKET, IS IT BETTER TO USE AN AGENT OR GO DIRECT?

It depends, going through an agency that has built a rapport with various entertainment buyers increases your chances of getting a gig. The don't have time to be searching for bands and rather go through an agency with an extensive roster. It becomes a "one stop shop". For local small club gigs and theaters, I don't think an agent is necessary. Me personally, I love getting a call from an artist directly that wants to book a show. It's a great way to establish a working relationship from the start instead of introducing ourselves to each other for the first time the night of the show.

WHAT TYPES OF MUSIC/ACTS DOES YOUR AGENCY SEE THE MOST DEMAND FOR?

(see answer to question 3)

ARE TRIBUTE ACTS A BETTER WAY TO GO THAN ORIGINAL MUSIC?

Well I'm partial to original bands. I love the idea of the passion, creativity, the heart and soul that goes into the whole creative process these artists dedicate to the craft and then watching them share it with an audience. It's incredibly exciting to be part of that experience. At the same time I understand the entertainment and nostalgic factor that is part of the tribute band scene.

IF MUSICIANS WANT TO CONTACT YOU REGARDING WORK, HOW SHOULD THEY DO IT?

ALL IN BLACK PRODUCTIONS at (805) 529-5884. We welcome unsolicited material. I am always looking for bands and artists looking to play and I'm really attracted to artists that step "outside the box". I love the edgy, provocative, and fresh stuff that some more "mainstream" producers might stay away from.

WHAT DO YOU LIKE TO SEE ON A VIDEO DEMO FROM A NEW ACT?

Energy, stage presence ... I have to be visually stimulated ... the stage is sacred ground and I love artists that treat it as such ... people have spent money to see you ... you have to deliver that "something special" that leaves people wanting more ... that should come across on the video ... Your video is selling your band and it should really "pop".

CAN YOU OFFER ANY STRATEGIES FOR LOCAL MUSICIANS TO GET THE BEST WORK?

Really work hard at building your fan base ... work on expanding your email list at every show ... really promote your shows and try to increase your draw ... It's hard for a promoter not to offer a gig to a band that draws ... word gets around ... if you are a band that is drawing well promoters find out. Once you get a good gig, be professional, be respectful of the venue and the staff ... let them know how much you would like to play there again ...

DO YOU HAVE ANY ADVISE FOR MUSICIANS JUST STARTING OUT IN THE BUSINESS?

Go to as many shows as you can. Check out your local scene and go out and meet people ... introduce yourself to the promoters, and anyone that may be involved with the production of shows. Offer to help out at shows ... learn the "behind the scene" stuff that goes into the production of a show. I also would encourage any artist to read books such as this to learn about the music business. There are so many wonderful resources such as DIY conferences, countless books, internet articles, other musicians you can talk to and learn things from. In addition to all this, believe in yourself and your talent. do it for the love of music ... and most importantly don't be seduced by the "lifestyle". Stay clean and focused and if you are able to achieve a measure of success be willing to give something back ... and always be appreciative of your fans ... never forget how important they are to your success.

APPENDIX

Sources

Here are some resources I find useful. This is not an exhaustive listing, you are encouraged to get on the internet and find books, articles, websites and videos that appeal to you or that have good reviews. Please also keep in mind that website addresses can change frequently. If you encounter an outdated link, simply type the information into the Google search engine and it should be easily found.

(*http://www.google.com*)

Books

Music Books Plus
http://www.musicbooksplus.com
ASCAP Book List
http://www.ascap.com/resource/resource-4.html

Selling Your Music—How to Sell Profitably Sell Your Own Music Online
http://www.nmdbooks.com

Websites—Lead Generation

Getting Signed—Books—Resource Site
http://www.getsigned.com/touring.html
Gigmasters
http://www.gigmasters.com
Directcatering—Gig Resource
http://www.directcatering.com
Powergig
http://www.powergig.com
Booklivemusic.com
http://www.booklivemusic.com

Videos

How To Find Gigs That Pay Big Bucks
http://www.musicbooksplus.com/books/byh01.htm

Musicians Contact Services

National Musicians Contact Service
http://www.musicianscontact.com

About The Author

Mark W. Curran is a Los Angeles-based musician, singer and author. Born and raised in Southeast Pennsylvania, he began playing paying gigs at the age of 16, and at the age of 20, joined the growing ranks of professional full time musicians touring the country. He would travel in road acts as a drummer and singer for the next decade on the infamous "Holiday Inn Circuit."

In 1987, he moved to Los Angeles, where he pursued a career in screenwriting and songwriting, while continuing to perform and write, eventually becoming a professional Elvis entertainer, embarking on his own "Elvis Across America" nationwide tour in 2002, winning critical reviews for his Elvis tribute act.

In 2003, he wrote and self-published his first book for musicians, "SELL YOUR MUSIC," and in 2005, self-published his second book, "GETTING GIGS," both books empowered musicians to fulfill their own destinies.

He continues to work and write music, while performing as a singer, lecturer and musician at small theaters and venues across the nation.

Other Books by Mark W. Curran

Sell Your Music Online!—The Musician's Survival Guide To Direct Distribution On The Internet.

You can order this book or additional copies of this book online at:

http://www.nmdbooks.com

or you may use the order form on next page:

Yes, please send me _____ copies of **"Sell Your Music Online!—The Musician's Survival Guide To Direct Distribution On The Internet,"** @ 19.95 each plus $4.95 domestic US shipping and handling. (Overseas or non-domestic please enclose $8.95 for shipping.) I am enclosing a check or money order made out to "NMD Books" in the amount of $_____.

My name and shipping address is:

Name _____

Street/Address _____

City/State/Zip _____

Please mail this order form to: NMD Books, 2828 Cochran St. Suite 285, Simi Valley, CA. 93065.

Lightning Source UK Ltd.
Milton Keynes UK
UKOW01f1923050216

267846UK00001B/101/P